The Most Sought-After Lost Treasures

Michael Harris
Editorial Anuket

Content

13.   The Sword of Joyeuse
Charlemagne's legendary sword, whose whereabouts were lost after the French Revolution. (47)
14.   The Treasure of Atahualpa
Gold was offered by the Inca emperor Atahualpa as a ransom to the Spanish conquistadors, and much of it was never found. (50)
15.   Blackbeard's Treasure
The booty of the famous pirate Blackbeard, supposedly buried on a Caribbean island. (53)
16.   The Florentine Jewel
A yellow diamond of great value disappeared after the First World War. (57)
17.   The Lost Dead Sea Scrolls
Some fragments of this ancient collection of biblical texts and apocrypha have not yet been located. (60)
18.   The crown of King John the Landless
Lost royal treasure of the English monarch, including the crown jewels, in the marshes of East Anglia in 1216. (63)
19.   The Treasure of the Caesars
Riches of the Roman Empire, many of which disappeared after the fall of Rome. (66)
20.   Marie Antoinette's necklace
Luxurious jewel associated with a famous scandal at the French court; Some of its pieces are believed to be missing. (69)
21.   The Golden Cross of the Battle of Bosworth
The relic is believed to have been carried by King Richard III during his last battle in 1485, lost after his defeat. (72)
22.   The Romanov Treasury
Jewelry, gold, and artifacts belonging to the Russian imperial family, disappeared after the 1917 Revolution. (74)
23.   Ali's Sword
Known as Zulfiqar, a legendary sword of Islam that is said to have been given by Muhammad. Its current location is unknown. (77)
24.   The Holy Grail and the Ark of the Covenant
The cup that, according to legend, Jesus Christ used at the Last Supper, has been searched for centuries, with multiple theories about its whereabouts; as well as the Ark, a biblical artifact that, according to tradition, contains the Tablets of the Law given to Moses. (80)
25.   The Treasure of San Juan Island
Riches that pirates are buried in the Virgin Islands. (87)

26.   The Treasure of the Golden Dolphins
Loot recovered from a shipwreck in the Caribbean, from which numerous gold pieces in the shape of dolphins are still missing. (91)

27.   The Chalice of Doña Urraca
A cup of gold and precious stones, supposedly linked to the Holy Grail, disappeared from a monastery in Spain. (95)

28.   Napoleon's Sword
One of the French emperor's swords was stolen during the nineteenth century and never recovered. (99)

29.   The Blue Diamond of Tavernier
Precursor of the famous Hope Diamond, this diamond disappeared after the French Revolution, and only a part of it was rediscovered. (103)

30.   The Nazi Gold Train
According to legend, a train loaded with gold and treasure disappeared in Poland at the end of World War II. Despite many searches, it has never been found. (107)

31.   The Art Theft of the Century
Several paintings by Rembrandt, including Christ in the Storm of the Sea of Galilee, were stolen in 1990 from the Isabella Stewart Gardner Museum in Boston, along with other priceless works of art. (111)

32.   Captain Kid's Treasure
Legends and mysteries of the most infamous pirate. (115)

Introduction

Throughout history, humanity has been driven by an innate desire to discover the hidden, to unearth that which has been lost in the shadows of time. From the fiery deserts of Egypt to the uncharted depths of the oceans, the most coveted treasures have left behind a trail of mystery, legend, and obsession.

In this book, "The Most Wanted Lost Treasures", we embark on a fascinating expedition through centuries of searching, intrigues, and secrets. Here you'll not only find objects of incalculable material value, such as pirate gold chests and jewels of vanished kings, but also relics whose meaning transcends the physical: artifacts that hold the key to lost cultures, manuscripts that could rewrite history, and sacred relics that promise to reveal spiritual truths.

Each chapter is a portal to an enigma that has not yet been solved. We will delve into the history of the Nazi gold train, chase the trail of the Holy Grail, and explore the abysses where pirate treasures are hidden. You'll hear from the stories of adventurers, treasure hunters, and looters, whose lives have been consumed by the search for these elusive objects.

But what drives someone to dedicate their life to pursuing a myth? Is it the desire for wealth, the craving for fame, or the seat of making sense of a world riddled with mysteries? Perhaps in the end, these treasures reveal something even more valuable: the eternal search of human beings to understand their place in the vast narrative of existence.

Get ready to immerse yourself in a journey where past and present intertwine, and where each page reveals secrets that have remained hidden for centuries. The treasures are there, waiting to be found. Do you dare to look for them?

1.   Yamashita's Treasure

Yamashita's treasure, also known as "Yamashita's Gold," is a legendary haul made up of huge amounts of gold, jewelry, and other valuables that were allegedly looted by the Japanese military during World War II. This priceless treasure would have been accumulated through plundering in occupied Asian countries such as China, Malaysia, Burma, and Indonesia, before being transported to the Philippines for temporary storage.

The legend takes its name from General Tomoyuki Yamashita, nicknamed "The Tiger of Malaysia," who commanded Japanese forces in the region. Although there is no conclusive evidence that Yamashita was directly involved in the operation, the myth has perpetuated his name as the unwitting guardian of this lost treasure.

Towards the end of the war, with Allied forces advancing, it is believed that the Japanese, fearing to lose control of the valuable loot, hid the treasure in complex networks of tunnels and caves in the Philippines. According to accounts, many of these caches were designed with death traps, such as explosives and sealed chambers, to protect the treasure and prevent its recovery.

Japan's defeat in 1945 left the supposed treasure in limbo. General Yamashita was captured and executed for war crimes, taking with him to his grave any knowledge he might have about gold. Since then, the story of the latter has captured the imagination of fortune seekers and has spawned countless expeditions.

Yamashita's Treasure hunts have been constant since the 1950s. Adventurers, treasure hunters, and private companies have dug at multiple locations in the Philippines in hopes of finding it. One of the best-known cases is that of Rogelio Roxas, a Filipino prospector who in the 70s claimed to have found part of the treasure: a gold statue of Buddha and chests full of gold ingots. However, Roxas was arrested, and his findings were allegedly confiscated by the regime of then-President Ferdinand Marcos.

This incident fueled conspiracy theories, suggesting that the treasure had been secretly recovered by senior government officials. To this day, Roxas' heirs have fought in international courts for compensation.

Among the hypotheses that are handled around his whereabouts are:

1. Hidden in tunnels and caves in the Philippines: The most widespread hypothesis suggests that the Yamashita Treasure remains hidden in the mountains and jungles of the Philippines, particularly in the Luzon region. The tunnels and caves allegedly used by the Japanese during the war were the perfect hiding place due to their inaccessibility and the difficulty of excavating them without advanced technology.

2. Recovered by the Philippine Government or Marcos: Another theory holds that the treasure was recovered in part or in whole by the Philippine government during the presidency of Ferdinand Marcos. Critics of the

regime allege that Marcos used the gold to finance his political and personal activities. However, there is no definitive evidence to support this claim.

3. Transported out of the Philippines: Some researchers believe that the Japanese managed to evacuate a significant portion of the treasure before the surrender, sending it back to Japan or even other parts of the world, where it could be stored in secret accounts or inaccessible hiding places.

4. An exaggerated legend: Finally, there is a possibility that the Yamashita Treasure is nothing more than an exaggerated legend or myth. While there are historical records of looting during the war, there is no conclusive evidence that such massive loot was gathered and hidden.

Interesting facts:

According to Rogelio Roxas, one of the most striking objects he found was a statue of Buddha made of solid gold, whose value was estimated at millions of dollars. This figure has become an icon in the history of Yamashita's Treasure.

The Roxas v. State of the Philippines case reached international courts, including a court in Hawaii, where the Roxas family received compensation, although the whereabouts of the treasure remain unclear.

Today, treasure hunts have turned to advanced technologies such as ground-penetrating radars and drones to scout out potential locations.

The cultural impact of Yamashita's Treasure:

Literature and Film: Films such as The Yamashita Treasure and documentaries produced by international networks such as National Geographic and the History Channel have explored history, further fueling the global fascination with this lost treasure.

Tourism and exploration: Some areas in the Philippines have seen an increase in tourism due to their association with the treasure legend. In addition, organized groups of explorers and treasure hunters conduct annual expeditions in search of clues.

Myth and reality: The Treasure of Yamashita has been compared to the Ark of the Covenant or the Holy Grail, in that it mixes elements of history, myth, and the human desire to unveil secrets of the past. Its persistence in popular culture reflects the human fascination with the unknown, and how, even in the modern world, legends of lost treasures continue to fuel the imagination.

Although Yamashita's Treasure remains one of the greatest enigmas in recent history, the lack of concrete evidence of its whereabouts has turned the search into something of a never-ending crusade for both the adventurers and the governments involved. The intervention of advanced technology, the testimony of former witnesses, and theories about the complicity of senior Philippine government officials only add more layers to the mystery.

Today, Yamashita's gold remains a symbol of greed, adventure, and mystery. The searches continue, but the treasure remains a ghost in the Philippine jungle, challenging those who dare to search for it and leaving an indelible mark on history.

2.   The Amber of the Amber Room: A Historical Enigma

The Amber Room was an extraordinary room of approximately 55 square meters, originally designed at the Charlottenburg Palace in Berlin during the eighteenth century. Initially created for King Frederick William I of Prussia, the room was completely covered with amber panels, a precious material formed by fossil resin that gave it an incomparable shine and decorative richness.

The panels were crafted from more than 6 tonnes of Baltic amber, combining intricate handcrafted designs with an estimated value at the time of several million euros today. Each panel was a true masterpiece, meticulously carved and decorated with sculptures, ornamental motifs, and a palette of shades ranging from golden yellow to deep orange.

In 1716, King Frederick William I gifted the hall to Tsar Peter the Great of Russia as a symbol of political alliance between Prussia and Russia. The room was moved to St. Petersburg, where it was installed in Catherine's Palace in Tsarskoye Selo, near the Russian capital.

For decades, the Amber Room was considered one of the most spectacular treasures of the European aristocracy, admired for its beauty and unique artistic value.

With the Nazi invasion of the Soviet Union in 1941, the museum's curators attempted to dismantle and protect the room. However, the German advance was so rapid that they only managed to cover the panels with paper and plaster.
The Nazis, aware of its historical value, completely dismantled the room and moved it to Königsberg (now Kaliningrad) to be exhibited in their local castle. This moment marks the beginning of the mystery about his final whereabouts.

There are multiple theories about what happened to the Amber Room after 1945:

Destruction during the bombings: Some historians suggest that it may have been destroyed during the Allied bombing raids on Königsberg.

Submarine sinking: There is a hypothesis that it was packed in boxes and transported in a German submarine that could have sunk in the Baltic Sea.

Secret hiding place: A group of researchers believe that it was hidden in bunkers or underground mines in present-day Polish or German territories.

Scattered fragments: Some research indicates that parts of the Amber Room may have been looted and distributed to private collectors.

In 1979, the Soviet Union began a reconstruction project based on historical photographs and existing documentation. After decades of work, a detailed replica was inaugurated in Catherine's Palace in 2003, symbolically restoring the splendor of this masterpiece.

Interesting Facts:

The amber used came mostly from the Baltic Sea region. It is estimated that the current value of the original room would exceed 250 million euros.

Multiple expeditions and research groups continue to search for clues to his whereabouts. Germany and Russia have collaborated on investigations to solve the mystery

The Amber Room remains one of the greatest mysteries of the world's cultural heritage. Its disappearance during the Second World War has made it a legendary treasure, a symbol of the conflicts and tragedies that marked the twentieth century.

The search continues, and in the meantime, its story continues to fascinate historians, collectors, and the public, reminding us that some treasures keep their enigma intact despite the passage of time.

3.   The Treasure of the Sad Night: Gold Lost in the Conquest of Mexico

The Treasure of the Sad Night refers to the riches looted by the Spanish conquistadors led by Hernán Cortés during the conquest of the Aztec Empire. This loot included gold, jewelry, precious stones, and artifacts of incalculable cultural value, largely obtained from the looting of the Palace of Moctezuma in Tenochtitlan.

The treasure became a deadly burden for the Spanish when, on the night of June 30 to July 1, 1520, the Aztecs rebelled and drove the conquistadors out of the city in an event known as La Noche Triste. During the frantic retreat, much of the loot was abandoned or lost in the canals and swamps surrounding the Aztec capital.

The conflict broke out after the death of Moctezuma II, whom the Aztecs held responsible for allowing the Spanish presence. The rebels besieged the conquistadors in Tenochtitlan, forcing them to flee amid a massive attack. Loaded with the booty, many Spanish soldiers and their Tlaxcalan allies fell while trying to cross the canals. Gold and jewelry that were not confiscated or hidden by the Aztecs sank into the mud and waters.

Hernán Cortés managed to reorganize his forces and eventually retook Tenochtitlan in 1521, marking the end of the Aztec Empire. However, much of the original treasure was never recovered, giving rise to a legend that endures to this day.

Since the 16th century, numerous expeditions have been made to locate the Treasure of the Sad Night. Explorers and historians have excavated ancient canals and archaeological sites in Mexico City, especially in areas such as Tacuba, where Cortés is believed to have mourned his defeat under a tree, now known as the Tree of the Sad Night.

In 1981, during the construction of the Mexico City metro, some valuables were found that some experts associated with the lost treasure. However, so far no significant amount of gold or other artifacts have been found to confirm the recovery of the mythical loot.

Hypotheses about his whereabouts:

1. Buried in the canals and swamps of Mexico City: A widely accepted theory is that the treasure remains buried under mud in what was once the canals of Tenochtitlan. Massive urbanization and the growth of Mexico City have complicated its location, but recent archaeological findings keep hope alive.

2. Hidden by the Aztecs: Some believe that the Aztecs managed to recover part of the treasure and hid it in sacred or remote places, far from the reach of the Spanish. This hypothesis suggests that the treasure could still be hidden in some unknown corner of the Valley of Mexico.

3. Dispersed and melted down by the Spanish: Another possibility is that the surviving Spaniards managed to take some of the booty with them, which was melted down and sent to Europe to finance the military campaigns of the Spanish crown.

4. Lost forever: The most pessimistic theory is that the treasure was destroyed or lost beyond recovery, either sunk in the mud or disintegrated by the passage of time and environmental conditions.

Interesting Facts:

The Tree of the Sad Night: Although the original tree where Cortés is said to have mourned his defeat died in 1980, its location remains an iconic place that attracts tourists and historians.

Archaeological findings: In 2020, a team of archaeologists found a gold bar in the historic center of Mexico City, which some believe could be part of the lost treasure.

Historical symbolism: Beyond its material value, the Treasure of the Sad Night symbolizes the tragedy and conflict between two civilizations, marking a turning point in the history of the Conquest of Mexico.

The Treasure of the Sad Night remains one of Mexico's great archaeological mysteries. The mix of history, myth, and legend that surrounds it has inspired generations of adventurers and scholars. While the search continues, each new finding brings humanity one step closer to unraveling one of the most fascinating enigmas of the conquest period.

4.   The Templar Treasure: Myth, History and Relentless Search

The Templar Treasure is one of the great mysteries of medieval history. The Knights Templar, a powerful military and religious order that emerged in the 12th century, are believed to have amassed a vast fortune during their campaigns in the Holy Land. This treasure would include gold, jewelry, sacred relics (such as the Holy Grail and the Spear of Destiny), ancient manuscripts, and even secrets that could change human history.

Beyond its material value, the Templar treasure is shrouded in a halo of mysticism. The Templars are said to have possessed esoteric knowledge and Christian relics of incalculable importance, fueling legends about their wealth and power.

The Knights Templar emerged in 1119 to protect Christian pilgrims in the Holy Land. Over time, the order became one of the most influential institutions in medieval Europe, amassing vast estates and wealth. Their banking and financial operations were precursors to modern systems, and many monarchs and nobles relied on them for the protection of their treasuries.

However, his power and wealth provoked envy. In 1307, King Philip IV of France, with the backing of Pope Clement V, ordered the dissolution of the order. Many Templars were arrested and executed, and their Grand Master, Jacques de Molay, was burned at the stake. Despite these efforts, much of the Templar fortune disappeared, giving rise to legends about a hidden treasure.

Since the dissolution of the order, numerous treasure hunters and historians have attempted to locate the mythical Templar treasure. Among the most explored places are:

1. The Fortress of Montségur, France: Considered a Templar stronghold, it is said that during the siege of Montségur, some Templars managed to flee with the treasure before the fall of the fortress.

2. Rosslyn Abbey, Scotland: Rosslyn Abbey is known for its intricate engravings and connection to the Templars. Some believe that its crypts hide Templar secrets and relics, including the Holy Grail.

3. Oak Island, Canada: One of the most intriguing theories suggests that the Templars brought their treasure to the New World centuries before Columbus arrived. Oak Island in Nova Scotia has been the subject of intense excavations due to alleged tunnels and shafts that could contain the treasure.

4. Temples and castles in Spain and Portugal: The Templars had a strong presence in the Iberian Peninsula. Castles such as Tomar in Portugal or Ponferrada in Spain have been investigated in search of clues about the treasure.

Hypotheses about his whereabouts:

1. Hidden in Europe: One of the most accepted hypotheses is that the treasure was hidden in multiple

secret locations by the Templars themselves, who anticipated the persecution. Some believe that he is buried in crypts, fortresses, or abbeys in France, Scotland, or Spain.

2. Transported to the New World: More recent theories suggest that the Templars may have sailed to America, depositing their treasure in places like Oak Island or even in remote areas of South America.

3. Incorporated into the Catholic Church: Another theory proposes that the treasure was absorbed into the Catholic Church after the dissolution of the order, which would explain the lack of tangible traces and the silence about its whereabouts.

4. Lost or destroyed: Finally, there is the possibility that much of the treasure was scattered, looted, or destroyed during the persecutions, being irretrievably lost to history.

Interesting facts:

Many legends link the Templars to the custody of the Holy Grail, the chalice used by Christ at the Last Supper. This artifact is considered one of the most valuable pieces of the Templar treasure.

Before dying at the stake, Grand Master Jacques de Molay allegedly cursed King Philip IV and Pope Clement V, who died soon after, fueling the mystique around the Templars.

Since the 18th century, the Isle of Oak has been the subject of excavations following the discovery of a mysterious well with signs of advanced engineering, which some associate with the Templar treasure.

The Templar Treasure has inspired numerous works of fiction, from The Da Vinci Code to Indiana Jones and the Last Crusade, reinforcing its place in popular culture.

The Templar Treasure continues to be a symbol of mystery, wealth, and power. Despite centuries of searching, their whereabouts remain an enigma, fueling the fascination with this medieval order and its legacy. Perhaps one day, an archaeological find can shed light on this legendary treasure and unveil one of history's best-kept secrets.

5.   Lima's Treasure: The Legend of a Loot Lost in the Ocean

The Treasure of Lima is one of the most legendary loots in history. It consists of a vast collection of riches that includes chests filled with gold and silver coins, jewelry, religious ornaments, chalices, crucifixes encrusted with gems, and a statue of the Virgin Mary made of pure gold, valued for her impressive artwork and devotion.

It is estimated that the treasure would have a current value of several hundred million dollars, but its true value lies in its historical and cultural significance, as it was a reflection of the immense power and wealth accumulated by the Catholic Church and the Spanish viceroyalty in Peru during the colonial era.

In 1820, during the Peruvian War of Independence, the situation in Lima became critical. With the imminent arrival of the independence forces under the command of General José de San Martín, the Spanish colonial authorities feared for the safety of the riches accumulated in the city. The decision was made to move the treasure to safety to prevent it from falling into insurgent hands.

The treasure was loaded onto the Mary Dear, a ship commanded by English Captain William Thompson. However, instead of fulfilling their mission to protect the riches, Thompson and his crew decided to seize the loot. According to the chronicles, they threw the religious guards overboard and sailed to an island in the Pacific, where they hid the treasure.

Soon after, Thompson and his crew were captured, but the captain refused to reveal the exact location of the loot. Although some accounts claim that he and a few companions managed to escape, the Lima Treasure was never recovered, giving rise to one of the world's most fascinating legends of lost treasures.

Lima's Treasure Hunt has attracted adventurers and treasure hunters for more than two centuries. The island most frequently mentioned as a possible hideout is Cocos, a remote island in the Pacific Ocean, about 550 kilometers southwest of Costa Rica.

Since the 19th century, numerous expeditions have been carried out to Cocos Island, using everything from traditional methods to modern technologies such as land-penetrating radars and submarines. However, none have managed to find conclusive evidence of the treasure.

The most popular theory places the treasure on this island, known for its caves, dense vegetation, and difficult access. It has been the focus of countless searches, but its rugged terrain and legal restrictions have limited efforts.

Another hypothesis suggests that Thompson may have taken the treasure to the less explored Galapagos Islands, with terrain equally conducive to hiding large quantities of gold and jewelry.

Some less popular theories point to more remote islands in the Pacific, including places like Hawaii or the Marquesas, although these lack concrete evidence.

The most widely accepted hypothesis is that the treasure remains buried in a secret cave or at the bottom of a bay on some Pacific island, waiting to be discovered.

Some believe that Thompson or his descendants may have returned to the hiding place and recovered the treasure, dispersing it later to avoid suspicion.

There is a possibility that the treasure has been destroyed or lost on the ocean floor, either due to tectonic movements, hurricanes, or geographical changes that have made it inaccessible.

Interesting facts:

The Treasure of Lima has served as the inspiration for multiple stories, including Robert Louis Stevenson's novel Treasure Island and adventure films such as Pirates of the Caribbean.

Cocos Island has been declared a UNESCO World Heritage Site, limiting treasure hunts, as the site is protected for its biodiversity and ecological significance.

Over the years, maps and journals have been discovered that allegedly belong to members of Thompson's crew, though many have been debunked as forgeries or frauds.

The Treasure of Lima continues to be one of the great enigmas of the world of lost treasures. Its history, full of betrayals, adventures, and mystery, continues to fascinate historians and adventurers. As modern technologies advance, perhaps one day this legendary loot will finally be discovered, revealing not only its immense material value but also a lost chapter of colonial history in Latin America.

6.   The Flying Dutchman's Loot: Myths and Mysteries of a Ghost Treasure

The Flying Dutchman's Booty is a legend that mixes the story of a ghost ship with a treasure lost on the high seas. According to tradition, the Flying Dutchman is a cursed galleon that, during a storm, disappeared without a trace while carrying an immense cargo of gold, silver, jewels, and spices from the East Indies.

The wealth on board was destined for the Dutch Crown, but the ship never reached its destination. It is said that the captain, in an act of defiance against God and nature, was condemned to wander eternally in the oceans, along with his crew and his treasure, becoming a symbol of greed and misery.

The legend of the Flying Dutchman has its roots in the seventeenth century, in the golden age of Dutch maritime trade. According to the myth, Captain Hendrik van der Decken commanded the ship. In 1641, while attempting to round the Cape of Good Hope, the ship was caught in a fierce storm.

Van der Decken, defying divine forces, vowed that he would complete his journey "even if it took him eternity." For this act of arrogance, both he and his ship were cursed, condemned to sail eternally without touching port.

The Flying Dutchman became a symbol of superstition for sailors. Over the centuries, there have been numerous sightings of a ghost ship, shrouded in fog and with torn sails, considered a bad omen by sailors.

Although the legend of the Flying Dutchman has a strong supernatural component, some adventurers believe that there could be a historical basis behind the story and that the lost loot could be real.

The place most associated with the Flying Dutchman is the Cape of Good Hope (Cape Town, South Africa). The treacherous waters and frequent storms in this region make it a logical site to look for the remains of an ancient shipwreck. However, no concrete evidence has been found of a ship matching the description of the Flying Dutchman.

Some theories propose that the ship may have been dragged south, sinking near the Falkland Islands. Underwater explorations have also been carried out here, without success.

Treasure hunters have speculated that the ship may have been wrecked in areas further north due to ocean currents. However, the vastness of the Atlantic and the lack of accurate records make any search difficult.

The most widely accepted theory is that the Flying Dutchman if it existed, sank near the Cape of Good Hope, a place known for its dangerous waters. Their loot could be buried under tons of marine sediment.

Another hypothesis holds that the Flying Dutchman is entirely fictional, a myth created to warn against human arrogance and the danger of defying natural forces. In this case, there would be no loot to look for.

Some theorize that, if the ship did indeed sink, its remains and cargo could be scattered in different places, making it virtually impossible to recover the treasure.

Interesting Facts:

One of the most well-known sightings of the Flying Dutchman occurred in 1881, when the crew of HMS Bacchante, including the future King George V, reported seeing a ghost ship off the coast of South Africa.

The legend of the Flying Dutchman has inspired numerous literary works, operas, and films, such as Pirates of the Caribbean: Dead Man's Chest, where it is mixed with other maritime myths.

The Flying Dutchman is a symbol of condemnation and the consequences of pride and unbridled greed, making it a timeless moral tale.

In recent years, technologies such as high-resolution sonar and underwater vehicles have been used to search for historic shipwrecks in the Cape region, though not specifically the Flying Dutchman.

The Flying Dutchman's Booty remains a fascinating mystery that combines naval history with maritime folklore. While there is no conclusive proof of its existence, the legend lives on in the collective imagination, inspiring those who seek to unravel the secrets of the sea and recover one of history's most legendary treasures.

7.   The Oak Island Treasure: The Mystery of the Money Pit

The Oak Island Treasure is one of the most enigmatic mysteries in modern history. Located on a small island off the coast of Nova Scotia, Canada, this treasure has become an object of fascination since the late 18th century. Its exact nature is unknown, but theories range from chests full of gold and jewels, to lost manuscripts of William Shakespeare or the Ark of the Covenant.

The alleged treasure is buried in a place known as the Money Pit, an engineering-defying structure equipped with flood tunnels designed to make it difficult to excavate.

The treasure's story began in 1795, when a young man named Daniel McGinnis found a strange sinkhole in the ground of Oak Island, accompanied by a pulley system in the nearby branches. Together with two friends, McGinnis began digging, finding layers of wood at regular intervals. As they advanced, they found a slab with mysterious inscriptions.

Since then, numerous search groups have attempted to unearth the treasure. However, each attempt has been met with flood tunnels that fill the well with seawater, halting excavations. Over the centuries, millions of dollars have been invested in the search, but the treasure continues to elude its hunters.

Early excavation efforts included companies such as the Onslow Company and the Truro Company in the 19th century. These organizations managed to advance several meters deep, but every time they approached the treasury, the tunnels were flooded.

In the twentieth century, figures such as Franklin D. Roosevelt, before becoming president of the United States, participated in the search. More recently, brothers Rick and Marty Lagina led a documented search in the television series The Haunting of Oak Island. They have used advanced technology, such as camera probes and large-scale excavations, to try to solve the mystery.

Over the years, intriguing artifacts have been found, such as a stone with unknown inscriptions, fragments of scrolls, and gold chains. However, none of these findings have been conclusive.

One of the most popular theories is that the treasure was buried by the famous pirate William Kidd or by Captain Blackbeard. Pirates were known to hide their riches on remote islands.

Another hypothesis, as we have already seen, suggests that the Money Pit was built by the Knights Templar and that it contains sacred relics, such as the Holy Grail or the Ark of the Covenant.

Some believe that the well could contain important historical documents, such as original manuscripts of Shakespeare or even evidence that would prove that Sir Francis Bacon was the true author of his works.

There is a possibility that the Money Pit is simply a geological formation or an ancient defense system and that it does not contain any significant treasure.

Interesting facts:

According to a local legend, seven people must die in the search before the treasure can be found. To date, six people have lost their lives in the expeditions.

The Money Pit is designed with a series of flood tunnels that are automatically activated. This level of sophistication suggests that whoever built the well had access to advanced engineering knowledge.

Oak Island has become a popular tourist destination, attracting thousands of people each year interested in the mystery.

The television series The Haunting of Oak Island has popularized the quest, introducing discoveries and theories each season.

The Oak Island Treasure remains an enigma that has captured the imagination of generations. Although some intriguing discoveries have been made, the mystery remains. Whether it's a pirate treasure, holy relics, or a clever hoax, the true story behind the Money Pit remains one of the great unsolved legends.

8.   Ivan the Terrible's Library: Russia's Lost Literary Treasure

The Library of Ivan the Terrible, also known as the Lost Library of Moscow or Liberia, is one of the most fascinating cultural mysteries in Russian history. According to legend, this collection contained hundreds, if not thousands, of rare manuscripts and ancient books, some coming from the Library of Constantinople after its fall in 1453.

Among the texts supposedly contained in this library were works of classical antiquity, Byzantine manuscripts, scientific treatises, theological writings, and Hermetic texts that were believed to be lost forever. Had it been preserved, it would have been one of the most important collections in the world, a veritable treasure trove of human knowledge.

The legend of the Library of Ivan the Terrible has its origins in the sixteenth century. According to various sources, Ivan's grandfather, Grand Duke Ivan III, was the one who initially assembled the collection, possibly inheriting it from Sophia Palaiologos, his wife and niece of the last Byzantine emperor. Sophie would have brought valuable books with her when she arrived in Moscow after the fall of Constantinople.

Ivan IV, known as Ivan the Terrible, would have inherited this collection and, according to the chronicles, expanded it with manuscripts from Asia and the Middle East. However, after the death of the Tsar in 1584, the library disappeared without a trace.

Since the 17th century, generations of researchers, archaeologists, and treasure hunters have searched for the Library of Ivan the Terrible in and around Moscow. Theories suggest that it could be hidden in tunnels, fortresses, or monasteries.

One of the most persistent theories is that the library is hidden in the tunnels under the Kremlin. This vast complex has been the subject of numerous excavations, but the search has been limited for security reasons and the fragility of the historic structures.

Another possible location is the Alexandrov Fortress, where Ivan the Terrible resided for part of his reign. The fortress has been excavated, but no conclusive evidence of the library has been found.

Some researchers believe that the collection was moved to distant monasteries during times of conflict to protect it from invaders. However, searches in these areas have not yielded definitive results either.

Many believe that the library is buried in secret chambers under the Kremlin, protected by a system of underground passageways built during Ivan's reign.

Some historians suggest that the library may have been destroyed in one of the numerous fires that devastated Moscow, particularly during the invasion of the Tatars or the Great Fire of 1812.

Another theory is that the library was looted during foreign invasions and its volumes are scattered around the world, in private collections or foreign libraries.

There is also the possibility that the library is simply a myth, a legend created to magnify the figure of Ivan the Terrible and the cultural richness of medieval Russia.

Interesting facts:

Some references to the library are found in historical documents that mention "secret books" and "hidden chambers" during the reign of Ivan IV.

In the 20th century, Soviet archaeologists carried out excavations in the Kremlin, using sonar technology to locate underground chambers. Although interesting structures were found, no remains of the library were found.

Ivan the Terrible's Library has inspired numerous works of literature and cinema, standing out as a symbol of Russia's lost cultural wealth.

If found, the library could rewrite some of the cultural and scientific history, providing access to lost works that could change our understanding of the past.

Ivan the Terrible's Library remains one of the greatest enigmas in history. Whether it's a real treasure or a myth perpetuated by centuries of speculation, its search continues to capture the imagination of explorers and scholars. If it exists, its discovery would be one of humanity's most important discoveries, revealing lost knowledge and expanding our understanding of past civilizations.

9. The Seal of Genghis Khan: The Lost Emblem of the Great Conqueror

The Seal of Genghis Khan is one of the most legendary objects associated with the founder of the Mongol Empire, Genghis Khan, who unified the Mongol tribes and conquered vast regions of Asia and Europe in the 13th century. This seal considered a symbol of supreme authority, would have been used to legitimize imperial decrees, designate leaders, and formalize political alliances.

Although no exact descriptions of the seal have been found, it is presumed that it was made of a precious material such as gold or jade, inscribed with Mongolian or Uyghur characters, and decorated with motifs representing the power of the Khan.

The Seal of Genghis Khan would have been forged during his reign, approximately between 1206 and 1227, and passed to his successors as a symbol of imperial continuity and authority. Its possession guaranteed the legitimacy of the ruler in the vast Mongol Empire, which at its height stretched from the Pacific to Central Europe.

However, following the fragmentation of the empire into several khanates and the subsequent fall of these states, the whereabouts of the seal were lost to history. It is believed that he may have been taken to Mongolia, China or even buried along with Genghis Khan, whose burial place also remains a mystery.

Over the centuries, archaeologists, historians, and treasure hunters have searched for the Seal of Genghis

Khan, considering that its finding would not only be a discovery of incalculable historical value but also an object of great symbolic importance.

Numerous searches have been carried out in the steppes of Mongolia, where it is believed that Genghis Khan may have been buried along with his treasures, including the seal. A key region is Burkhan Khaldun Mountain, a sacred site mentioned in ancient chronicles.

Karakorum, the former capital of the Mongol Empire has been another focus of exploration. Although significant artifacts have been found, the seal remains elusive.

Since China was a central region in the empire and the Yuan Dynasty was directly descended from Genghis Khan, some believe that the seal could have been carried there and hidden somewhere during the fall of the dynasty.

The most popular hypothesis is that the seal is buried next to the Great Khan in an unknown location. According to legends, his tomb was deliberately hidden to protect it from looters.

Another theory suggests that the seal was lost or destroyed during the civil wars and fragmentation of the Mongol Empire in the 14th century.

Some believe that the seal may have been protected by a noble family or kept in a monastery, waiting to be rediscovered.

There are conspiracy theories that claim that the stamp could be in the hands of a private collector, who keeps its existence a secret due to its immense historical and cultural value.

Interesting facts:

The exact location of Genghis Khan's tomb remains one of the greatest archaeological enigmas. Mongolian tradition prevents digging at sacred sites, which has limited research.

The Khan's tomb is also believed to contain weapons, armor, and other symbols of power.

At its peak, the Mongol Empire was the largest contiguous empire in history, making any artifacts from this era of exceptional historical value.

The seal represented the central authority and unity of the vast empire, uniting diverse cultures and ethnicities under Mongol rule.

The Seal of Genghis Khan remains an object of legend, a lost symbol that encapsulates the power and grandeur of the Mongol Empire. His search continues to fascinate archaeologists and historians, who hope his discovery will shed light on the life and legacy of one of history's most influential conquistadors. Until it is found, the seal will remain one of the most sought-after and enigmatic treasures in the world.

10.   The Treasure of the Flower of the Sea: The Fortune Lost in the Ocean

The Flor de la Mar (Flower of the Sea in Portuguese) was a luxurious and robust Portuguese carrack of the sixteenth century, famous for carrying one of the greatest riches of the time: a cargo of gold, jewelry, spices, and other treasures looted in Malacca (present-day Malaysia). This treasure was intended to enrich the court of King Manuel I of Portugal, becoming a symbol of the expansion and power of the Portuguese Empire during the Age of Discovery.

The estimated value of the Flor de la Mar's treasure amounts to billions of dollars today, making it one of the most coveted and mysterious loots in history.

Built in 1502, the Flor de la Mar was one of the largest carracks of its time. Initially, the ship played a crucial role in Portuguese maritime expansion, sailing to India and other regions of Southeast Asia.

In 1511, Alfonso de Albuquerque, governor of the Portuguese possessions in Asia, led the conquest of Malacca, one of the most important port cities in the region. After sacking the city, Albuquerque loaded the Flor de la Mar with untold treasure, including:

- Gold and silver collected from local sultanates.
- Precious jewelry, including unique gems.
- Rare spices from the region, highly valued in Europe.

On her way back to Portugal, the Flor de la Mar encountered a fierce storm in the Strait of Malacca. The ship was wrecked in 1511, and its valuable cargo sank to the bottom of the sea. Although Albuquerque and some crew survived, the treasure was never recovered.

The Flor de la Mar has captured the imagination of treasure hunters, historians, and archaeologists for centuries. Despite advances in underwater search technology, their exact whereabouts remain an enigma.

The Strait of Malacca is one of the busiest sea passages in the world, but also one of the most dangerous due to its unpredictable currents and shallow waters. Numerous expeditions have attempted to locate the remains of the Flor de la Mar, but conditions and the vast search area have complicated the efforts.

In recent decades, explorers have used side-scanned sonar, remotely operated vehicles (ROVs), and magnetometers to locate the wreck. However, the presence of numerous shipwrecks in the region has made precise identification difficult.

The most widely accepted theory is that the Flor de la Mar lies at the bottom of the Strait of Malacca, covered by centuries of sediment and surrounded by other shipwrecks.

Some researchers suggest that the ship may have been displaced by the strong currents of the strait, away from the original site of the wreck.

There is speculation that parts of the treasure may have been recovered by local fishermen or looters in centuries past, leaving only scattered fragments of the original cargo.

Given the difficult conditions, some experts believe that the treasure could remain lost forever, protected by the depths of the sea.

Interesting facts:

The treasure of the Flor de la Mar is said to include gifts intended for the King of Portugal, such as a solid gold throne and unique pieces of jewelry.

Despite numerous recovery attempts, no confirmed finds of the Flor de la Mar have been reported, keeping the legend alive.

The shipwreck has inspired books, documentaries, and films, cementing its place as one of history's most sought-after lost treasures.

Interest in the treasure has led to tensions between Indonesia, Malaysia and Portugal, all claiming a historical link to the wreck.

The Sea Flower and its lost treasure continue to be a symbol of the ambition, wealth, and mystery of the Age of Discovery. If it is ever found, it will not only represent one of the greatest archaeological finds in history, but also a cultural legacy that could rewrite entire chapters of the maritime past. Until then, the treasure remains an elusive dream, hidden in the depths of the sea.

11. The Irish Crown Jewels: The Mystery of an Unsolved Robbery

The Irish Crown Jewels, also known as the Insignia of the Order of St. Patrick, were a set of ceremonial objects of great value and historical significance. Included:

•   St. Patrick's Star: A gold star encrusted with diamonds.
•   The Grandmaster's Badge: A brooch with rubies, sapphires and diamonds.
•   Necklaces of the Order of St. Patrick: Made of gold, each adorned with thirteen roses enameled in white and red, interspersed with green clovers.

These objects were used by members of the Order of St. Patrick, an order of chivalry established in 1783 by King George III. They symbolized British prestige and authority in Ireland during the period of English rule.

The jewels were commissioned in 1831 to replace an earlier set, which had been removed. For years, they were stored in the Dublin Chamber, in Dublin Castle, which served as the seat of British power in Ireland.

On July 6, 1907, the Irish Crown Jewels were stolen from their display case in the Dublin Chamber. The crime was discovered when the deputy keeper inspected the room and noticed that the safe was open and the jewelry was missing.

The theft was extremely controversial due to alleged security negligence. The safe where the jewelry was kept was not properly locked, and some reports suggested that the keys were accessible.

Since the time of the theft, the Irish crown jewels have been the subject of intense investigations and speculation, but have never been recovered.

The initial investigation was fraught with controversy. Someone with internal access to the castle was suspected of having committed the theft. The main suspects included Sir Arthur Vicars, the then-keeper, who was charged with negligence. Although Vicars always claimed his innocence, he was removed from office and his reputation was ruined.

Theories about the fate of the jewels range from the involvement of Irish independence groups to a political conspiracy to discredit British officials. Some even suggested that the jewelry was sold on the black market or hidden somewhere in Ireland.

Despite advances in tracking technology and archaeology, the Irish Crown Jewels remain missing. On several occasions, searches of private property and land in Dublin have been carried out, but without success.

One popular theory is that the jewels remain hidden somewhere in Ireland, possibly buried or stored in an unknown location.

Another possibility is that the jewels were disassembled and sold separately on the black market, which would make it difficult to trace them.

Some believe that the jewels could be in the hands of a private collector who is unaware of their origin or who keeps them secret due to their illegal provenance.

Although less likely, there is a chance that the jewelry may have been destroyed, melted down, or discarded to prevent recovery.

Interesting facts:

In addition to their material value, the Irish Crown Jewels have immense historical and symbolic value, representing a turbulent period in the relationship between Ireland and Great Britain.

Vicars' life was ruined by the scandal. In 1921, he was assassinated during the Irish War of Independence, an act possibly related to his alleged links with the British.

More than a century after the robbery, the case remains unsolved, becoming one of the greatest mysteries in Irish history.

The Irish Crown Jewels have been the subject of numerous books, documentaries, and research programs.

The theft of the Irish Crown Jewels is a fascinating and enigmatic chapter in history. This mystery continues to intrigue historians, researchers, and treasure hunters. Can the jewels ever be found, or will they remain forever hidden, fueling legends and speculation? Time will tell.

12.   The Treasure of La Galga: A Mystery Buried in Maritime History

The Treasure of La Galga refers to the riches allegedly carried on board the Spanish frigate La Galga, a warship that was shipwrecked off the coast of Virginia, United States, in 1750. According to legend, the ship was carrying a valuable cargo of gold, silver, jewels, and other valuables from the Spanish Empire.

Although the true extent of the treasure is still debated, it is believed that the ship was carrying goods and precious metals intended to finance Spanish colonial efforts in the New World.

The Galga set sail in 1750 from Havana, Cuba, bound for Spain. However, during her crossing of the Atlantic, she encountered a violent storm that pushed her towards the coast of Virginia. On September 5, 1750, the frigate ran aground on Assateague Island, near the modern city of Chincoteague, Virginia, USA.

Although the crew managed to survive and reach shore, the ship and its cargo were trapped in the shallows. The frigate deteriorated over time, while the sand and sea hid its remains.

The shipwreck of La Galga is an integral part of local folklore in the Chincoteague region. One of the most famous stories is that the island's wild horses are descended from the animals that survived the shipwreck of the Spanish ship. Although this theory has been challenged, it remains a central element of the area's cultural legacy.

For centuries, La Galga has fascinated the attention of historians, treasure hunters, and archaeologists. However, finding the ship's wreck has proved to be a monumental challenge due to changing geographical conditions and the inaccurate nature of historical records.

In the 1980s, a treasure hunter named Barry Clifford set out on an expedition to locate La Galga. Using historical records and sonar technology, Clifford claimed to have found the ship's wreckage buried under the island's sand. However, details about the discovery and possible recovery of the treasure remain controversial.

The search for and recovery of historic shipwrecks in the United States is regulated by federal and state laws, which has led to legal disputes between private explorers and government authorities. In the case of La Galga, the Spanish government has also claimed rights to any treasure recovered, further complicating the situation.

The most widely accepted theory is that La Galga and its treasure remain buried under the dunes of the island of Assateague, hidden by centuries of sedimentation.

Some experts suggest that the treasure may have been scattered by ocean currents, scattering the valuables over a large area of the ocean floor.

Another possibility is that the treasure was looted shortly after the wreck by locals or even the surviving crew themselves, leaving little to nothing to be found.

Interesting facts:

The shipwreck of La Galga has inspired numerous stories and books, standing out as one of the most fascinating maritime stories on the East Coast of the United States.

The connection between La Galga and wild horses continues to be a topic of debate and fascination, attracting tourists and nature lovers.

Clifford's claims about the La Galga find have been met with skepticism by some archaeologists, who insist on the need for stronger evidence.

The Treasure of La Galga is a mixture of history, legend, and mystery. Although the remains of the frigate and its precious cargo remain hidden, the search continues to capture the imaginations of explorers and curious alike. If it is ever discovered, it will not only solve a mystery of more than two centuries but also shed light on a fascinating chapter of Spanish and American maritime history.

13.   The Sword of Joyeuse: The Legendary Weapon of the Kings of France

The Sword of Joyeuse is one of the most famous and legendary weapons in medieval history, considered to be the symbol of royalty and the power of the kings of France. The sword is believed to have been a sacred relic, used in the coronation of French monarchs for centuries.

The Joyeuse Sword is characterized by its blade decorated with intricate details and its hilt adorned with gems and precious metals. The sword is known to have a gold hilt and blade that reflected the prestige of its wielder. In addition, the sword possessed great symbolic importance: it was not only an instrument of war, but also an object of divine power, linked to the legitimacy of the monarch and his ability to rule under the protection of God.

The history of the Sword of Joyeuse is surrounded by mystery and legend, being a symbol of the French monarchy since the Middle Ages.

The exact origin of the sword is uncertain, but it is believed to have been forged in the ninth century, possibly during the reign of Charlemagne, the emperor of the Franks. According to some versions, the sword was given to Charlemagne by the Byzantine emperor himself, who considered it a symbolic gift for the most powerful leader of the Christian West. In other legends, the sword is said to have been forged by a divine blacksmith, giving the sword a mystical aura that linked it to the fate of the kings of France.

The Sword of Joyeuse was used in the coronations of French monarchs for more than a thousand years. Tradition was that the sword was given to the new king during the coronation ceremony, as a sign of his authority. The sword became one of the most important symbols of royal sovereignty and was said to have been used by several of France's most prominent kings, including Louis XIV, the "Sun King".

Over the centuries, the Sword of Joyeuse has been the subject of theft, loss, and mystery. Currently, his whereabouts are unknown, which has generated numerous theories and searches.

The last time the Sword of Joyeuse is known to have been used in a royal coronation was in the 14th century, during the reign of Charles VI of France. After this date, the sword disappeared from historical records. Some historians believe that the sword was stolen or lost during the tumultuous years of the Hundred Years' War, while others maintain that it was hidden due to its religious and political symbolism.

In the 16th century, the sword was thought to have been taken to the Louvre Museum, but its exact location could not be confirmed. Over the years, some have speculated that the sword might have been hidden in private collections or held by other monarchs, but no official record has confirmed its whereabouts.

In more recent times, archaeologists and medieval history experts have attempted to track down the sword, but so far no definitive proof has been found about its location. Searches of the Louvre and other institutions have yielded few results, and historical records remain vague and contradictory.

One of the most popular theories is that the Sword of Joyeuse was destroyed or lost during the French Revolution (1789-1799) when revolutionaries destroyed many of the symbols of the monarchy. If the sword was destroyed around this time, its existence would vanish without a trace.

Another theory suggests that the sword could be hidden in the depths of the Louvre Museum in Paris or some other secret collection. In some historical documents, it is mentioned that the sword was kept in the museum during the French Revolution to protect it from looting, leading to speculation that it might be in a secret vault.

Other historians think that the sword may have been removed from circulation and hidden in a noble family, out of reach of the French monarchs. This hypothesis suggests that the sword was kept secret, waiting for the right moment to be presented again as a symbol of power.

Interesting facts:

The name Joyeuse translates to "joy" or "happiness" in French, a name that reflects the hope of kings upon being crowned with it.

The sword was believed to have magical and divine powers. According to some legends, whoever wielded the Sword of Joyeuse would be blessed with success and victory in his battles.

Today, the Louvre Museum houses a replica of the Sword of Joyeuse that is on display as part of the collection of French historical artifacts, although it is not known if it is an accurate replica or if it was forged more recently to symbolize the original sword.

The Sword of Joyeuse is a key piece of French history, a symbol of power, divinity, and monarchy. Its mysterious disappearance has only increased its appeal as a lost treasure of great historical value. While the search for his whereabouts continues, the sword remains a legacy that remains in legends and the collective imagination, representing the greatness of the French monarchy and the undiscovered secrets of its past.

14. Atahualpa's Treasure: The Golden Legend of the Inca Empire

The Atahualpa Treasure is one of the most fascinating and coveted mysteries in South American history. This legendary treasure consists of a vast collection of gold, silver, and jewelry, which is believed to have been gathered by the Inca people to pay the ransom of their emperor Atahualpa, captured by the Spanish conquistadors led by Francisco Pizarro in 1532.

The treasure included objects of great cultural value, such as gold vessels, statues of divinities, ceremonial ornaments, and silver plates, all worked with the craftsmanship that characterized the Inca Empire.

Atahualpa, the last emperor of the Inca Empire, was captured in the city of Cajamarca after Pizarro's ambush. To negotiate his release, Atahualpa offered to fill a room about 6 meters long by 5 meters wide with gold up to a height of approximately 2.5 meters, and the same with silver in two additional rooms. The Incas began to gather ransom, sending valuable pieces of gold and silver from all over the empire.

Even though much of the ransom was delivered, Pizarro, fearing an Inca uprising and under pressure from his men, executed Atahualpa in 1533. After his death, the promise of the ransom was left incomplete. According to legends, the objects that did not reach Cajamarca were hidden by the Incas in remote places to prevent them from falling into Spanish hands.

It is estimated that more than 6 tons of gold and 12 tons of silver were melted down and distributed among the conquistadors. However, a large part of the rescue was never found, starting the legend of a lost treasure.

Since the 16th century, explorers and adventurers have been trying to locate the lost treasure. The most sought-after regions include the mountainous and jungle areas of the Andes, such as Vilcabamba, the last refuge of the Inca resistance, and the Amazon rainforest, where it is believed that the Incas might have hidden their riches.

One of the most popular theories is that the treasure was hidden in the remote and dangerous mountains of Llanganates, in Ecuador. According to accounts, the Inca general Rumiñahui would have transported and hidden the riches in this area to protect them from the conquerors.

In the 20th and 21st centuries, numerous expeditions have been carried out with advanced technology, including ground-penetrating radar and drones. Although objects and structures have been found that could be related to the Inca culture, Atahualpa's great treasure continues to elude searchers.

The most widely accepted theory is that the treasure remains hidden somewhere in the Llanganates Mountains, a hard-to-reach place known for its rugged terrain, unpredictable weather, and thick vegetation.

Some historians suggest that the treasure may have been divided and hidden in multiple locations throughout the Inca Empire, which would explain why it has not been found in its entirety.

Another less common but intriguing hypothesis is that some of the treasure may have been found in secret by treasure hunters, who chose not to disclose their findings to avoid legal disputes or government claims.

Interesting facts:

Beyond its material value, the treasure represents an invaluable cultural legacy. The objects could provide information about the Incas' life, beliefs, and artistic abilities.

Like many lost treasures, Atahualpa's is surrounded by tales of curses and misfortunes that affect those who seek it, adding a mystical element to the legend.

The treasure has inspired numerous books, documentaries, and films, fueling the dream of modern explorers and adventurers.

The Treasure of Atahualpa remains one of the great unsolved historical mysteries. Their search represents not only the hope of finding material riches but also the desire to unravel a crucial part of the history of the Inca Empire. As long as the treasure remains hidden, it will continue to fuel imagination and expeditions in search of one of the most legendary loots in the world.

15. Blackbeard's Treasure: The Gold Legend of the Caribbean's Most Famous Pirate

Blackbeard's Treasure refers to the alleged accumulation of riches that the infamous pirate Edward Teach, known as Blackbeard, would have looted and hidden during his years of activity in the Caribbean. This treasure is mainly composed of Coins, ingots, and precious metal objects obtained through the looting of merchant ships and colonies. Necklaces, rings, earrings, and precious stones were stolen from the victims. Artifacts, navigational tools, and other valuable items used in the pirate life.

The estimated value of Blackbeard's treasure is incalculable, not only for its material value but also for its historical and cultural significance as a symbol of the golden age of piracy in the Caribbean.

Edward Teach, better known as Blackbeard, was one of the most feared and legendary pirates of the eighteenth century. Born in England around 1680, Blackbeard joined the pirate life and quickly became noted for his audacity and strategic skill. His nickname, "Blackbeard," comes from his intimidating appearance: a bushy, often braided black beard, accompanied by strips of burning cloth that created a terrifying atmosphere during fighting.

Blackbeard commanded the ship Queen Anne's Revenge, one of the most powerful pirate ships of its time. With this vessel, he attacked numerous European merchant ships, accumulating a great deal of wealth. Blackbeard's treasure is estimated to have consisted of hundreds of thousands of pounds in gold and silver, in addition to jewelry and other valuables he acquired during his raids.

Blackbeard's fortunes came to an end in November 1718, when he was ambushed and killed by the British Navy led by Lieutenant Robert Maynard in a battle near Ocracoke, North Carolina. During this engagement, Queen Anne's Revenge was badly damaged and wrecked off the shores of the island, which could have contributed to the scattering and concealment of the treasure.

Since his death, Blackbeard's treasure legend has inspired numerous treasure hunters, archaeologists, and adventurers to undertake searches in the Caribbean and beyond. Expeditions have focused primarily on areas where the Queen Anne's Revenge is believed to have been shipwrecked, as well as nearby islands that could have served as treasure hideouts.

Immediately after the shipwreck, fishermen and locals attempted to recover what was left of the ship, though with little success due to adverse sea conditions and a lack of advanced technology.

Ancient documents and maps have been used to attempt to locate the exact wreck of the Queen Anne's Revenge, although estimates vary considerably.

With the advent of side-scan sonar, remotely operated vehicles (ROVs), and advanced diving techniques, searches have been more precise, although the treasure has yet to be found.

Teams of marine archaeologists have conducted multiple expeditions in search of the wreck and treasure, uncovering minor artifacts, but without locating the main loot.

Although the main treasure remains unfound, some expeditions have identified remains of Queen Anne's Revenge and recovered objects belonging to the ship, such as anchors, weapons, and pieces of furniture. These findings have helped confirm the shipwreck's overall location, but the treasure trove of gold and jewels remains hidden.

The most widely accepted hypothesis is that the treasure is found at the site of the shipwreck of the Queen Anne's Revenge. The current conditions of the seafloor, with strong currents and sediments, could have protected the treasure from being discovered until now.

It is also possible that, after the shipwreck, some of the treasure was scattered by the crew or by subsequent looters, making it difficult to locate it entirely in one place.

Others believe that Blackbeard may have hidden a portion of his treasure on nearby islands or in underwater caves before the shipwreck to protect him from enemy attacks.

Another theory suggests that some of the treasure was recovered and confiscated by the British navy after Blackbeard's defeat, stored in military arsenals, or distributed among the officers.

Interesting facts:

Blackbeard has been romanticized in popular culture as the ultimate pirate, with depictions in movies, books, and urban legends adding to the appeal of his lost treasure.

Queen Anne's Revenge is not only famous for its captain but also for its size and might, being one of the most imposing pirate ships of its time.

Blackbeard's treasure hunt has inspired numerous TV shows, documentaries, and books, keeping the fascination with this enigmatic loot alive.

Ocracoke Island where Blackbeard was shot down is now a tourist spot that offers tours and activities related to the pirate, attracting those looking to connect with the treasure's history.

Beyond its material value, the treasure represents the opulence and scope of piracy in the Caribbean, as well as stories of resistance and survival in a time of constant maritime conflict.

Blackbeard's Treasure remains one of the most captivating mysteries in the history of piracy. Despite numerous expeditions and technological advances, the wealth hidden by one of the Caribbean's most iconic pirates remains undiscovered. This mystery not only attracts treasure hunters but also fuels the imagination of entire generations fascinated by legends of gold and adventures on the high seas. While the Caribbean Sea holds its secrets, Blackbeard's treasure remains a golden promise waiting to be revealed.

16. The Florentine Jewel: A diamond of legend

The Florentine Jewel is a Renaissance-cut yellow diamond that stands out for its unique size, color, and cut. Originally known as the Grand Duke of Tuscany, this extraordinary diamond has been one of the most fascinating and mysterious gems in history.

Key features:

Weight: Approximately 137.27 carats, which placed it among the largest diamonds in the world.

Color: Light yellow with green tones and a distinctive shine.

Size: Carved in the shape of a rose with nine symmetrical faces, it represented the mastery of the Renaissance lapidary.

Origin: According to legends, the diamond came from the Golconda mines in India, famous for producing some of the most iconic gems in the world.

The Florentine Jewel first appeared in historical records in the 17th century. It is believed to have been acquired by the powerful Medici family, rulers of Florence, and great patrons of Renaissance art. The gem was cut and worn as a symbol of the power, wealth, and sophistication of this dynasty.

After the extinction of the Medici male line in 1737, the diamond passed into the hands of the House of Habsburg through Maria Theresa I, who incorporated it into the Austrian imperial treasury. During this period, the gem was used in crowns, scepters, and other royal jewelry, cementing its reputation as a symbol of the European monarchy.

The fate of the Florentine Jewel changed drastically after the fall of the Austro-Hungarian Empire in 1918. Following the abdication of Emperor Charles I, the diamond was taken to Switzerland along with other imperial treasures. However, amid chaos and political reorganization, the jewel disappeared without a trace. It is presumed that it was stolen or sold on the black market to finance political or personal activities.

The disappearance of the Florentine Jewel has given rise to countless theories, investigations, and searches around the world. To this day, the gem remains one of the most coveted and enigmatic diamonds.

It is believed that the diamond may have been split into smaller gems to make it difficult to identify. These pieces could have been sold and scattered all over the world.

Some speculate that the original gem could be intact in the hands of a private collector, who keeps it hidden due to its controversial origin and priceless value.

The disappearance in Switzerland suggests that it may have been stolen by someone with access to the imperial treasury. Since then, the diamond could have been moved to different countries.

Interesting facts:

The Florentine Jewel is not only valuable for its size and rarity but also for its association with the Medici, one of the most influential families of the Renaissance.

In some ancient texts, similar jewelry is mentioned, which has led to confusion about the exact identity of the diamond and its whereabouts.

If the Florentine Jewel were to reappear today, its market value would exceed hundreds of millions of dollars, considering its history and rarity.

The gem has inspired novels, documentaries, and movies speculating about its fate, fueling global fascination with this mysterious piece.

The Florentine Jewel is more than a diamond; It is a symbol of the wealth, power, and secrets of the great European dynasties. Although missing for more than a century, its legend persists as a reminder of the human fascination with treasures and historical mysteries. Is it hidden somewhere in the world, waiting to be rediscovered? The search for this unique gem continues, captivating historians, collectors, and adventurers alike.

17.   The Lost Dead Sea Scrolls: A Mystery to Be Solved

The Dead Sea Scrolls are a collection of ancient texts that contain some of the most important documents related to Judaism and early Christianity. Written in Hebrew, Aramaic, and Greek, they are estimated to date between the third century B.C. and the first century A.D.

Its content includes biblical books, religious commentaries, apocalyptic texts, community rules, and secular documents. Their inscriptions are presented on parchments, papyrus, and even copper. They were found in caves near the Dead Sea in Qumran by Bedouin herders in 1947.

While most of the known manuscripts are in academic collections and museums, there is an unknown number of texts that have been lost or remain hidden since their discovery.

The first scrolls were discovered by chance, leading to an archaeological search that revealed more than 900 manuscripts in 11 caves. The collection included old copies of biblical books and texts that illuminated the religious and social practices of the time.

After the discovery, many manuscripts were sold in antiquities markets without rigorous controls. Some complete or fragmented texts were acquired by private collectors and never officially registered, which caused part of this historical legacy to be lost.

During the 1950s and 1960s, unauthorized prospectors ransacked additional caves in search of texts. This resulted in the disappearance of many fragments that were sold illegally or destroyed due to inadequate storage conditions.

The possibility that undiscovered or missing manuscripts exist remains an enigma that attracts archaeologists, historians, and treasure hunters.

Some believe that the lost manuscripts are hidden in unexplored caves in the Qumran region because it is vast and difficult to access. It is believed that there could be more caves containing as-yet-undiscovered texts, protected from time and the elements.

Others maintain that they were fragmented and sold. Many small, hard-to-identify fragments have been sold in antique markets and are scattered in private collections.

Some manuscripts may have disintegrated due to humidity and extreme desert conditions.

It is also possible that significant fragments are in the hands of collectors who do not understand their importance or are afraid to reveal them for legal reasons.

During the first few years after their discovery, some fragments were poorly documented or classified, which could mean that they are in unidentified collections.

Interesting facts:

In 2017, archaeologists discovered a new cave at Qumran (dubbed Cave 12) that contained evidence of looted manuscripts, reinforcing the idea that more lost texts exist.

Some fragments have appeared at international auctions, leading to controversy over their authenticity and provenance.

Part of the original manuscripts includes a text engraved in copper that mentions hidden treasures, adding a layer of mystery to the lost manuscripts.

Not only are these texts crucial to understanding religious history, but they also offer invaluable context about Judaism and the origins of Christianity.

The Lost Dead Sea Scrolls are one of the greatest archaeological and cultural enigmas of our time. While some fragments remain hidden, their search remains a priority for archaeologists and historians who wish to complete this priceless puzzle. Each rediscovered fragment not only sheds light on the past but also connects us to the roots of civilization and spiritual thought. Are they hidden in remote caves, stored in private collections, or lost forever? The mystery continues.

18.   The crown of King John the Landless: A jewel lost in history

The Crown of King John the Landless is one of the most intriguing jewels of the English monarchical legacy. Although it is not known exactly what it looked like, it is presumed that it was made of precious metals, such as gold, and adorned with gems, reflecting the wealth and power of the medieval monarch. This crown symbolized the divine right of kings and their authority over the kingdom.

Presumptive features:
Materials: Gold, pearls, and precious stones typical of the time, such as rubies, emeralds, and sapphires.

Design: Based on medieval styles, probably with arches and a cross, like other English royal crowns.

Beyond its material value, the crown has cultural and political significance, as it belonged to one of England's most controversial kings.

John I of England, nicknamed John the Landless, reigned from 1199 to 1216. His reign was marked by disputes with the nobility, territorial losses in France and clashes with the Pope. He is best known for his role in signing the Magna Carta in 1215, which limited royal power and established the basic rights of subjects. He received that nickname because being the youngest son of King Henry II of England and Eleanor of Aquitaine, he did not receive a large inheritance.

In 1216, during a military campaign against the rebellious barons and their French allies, John undertook a journey through eastern England. According to the chronicles, while crossing the treacherous marshes of The Wash, an area of floodable lowlands, his royal luggage was lost in a flash flood. This luggage included royal treasures, jewels, and supposedly the king's crown.

The crown's demise has intrigued historians, archaeologists, and treasure hunters for centuries. Although no conclusive evidence has been found, legends about the loss of the treasure at The Wash have inspired numerous searches.

Many believe the crown and the rest of the treasure remain buried in The Wash, covered in mud and sand after centuries of tides and sedimentation.

Another theory suggests that the valuables were looted by locals after the accident and the crown was dismantled to sell the precious stones and gold.

Since England was at war with France, some speculate that French spies or allies may have recovered the treasure and brought the crown to the continent.

It is possible that, if it was recovered, the crown was melted down or destroyed during the tumultuous medieval period.

Interesting facts:

According to medieval chronicles, John was deeply affected by the loss of his treasure. Shortly after the incident, he died of dysentery, leaving his kingdom in turmoil.

Numerous archaeological expeditions and unauthorized searches with metal detectors have attempted to locate the treasure in The Wash. However, the changing terrain makes it difficult to locate any remains.

The loss of King John's crown and treasure has inspired historical and fictional accounts, from novels to conspiracy theories.

The disappearance of the crown has been interpreted as a symbol of the fall of the absolute power of monarchs, especially at a time when King John was forced to accept limits on his authority.

The Crown of King John the Landless is more than a lost jewel; It is emblematic of a tumultuous period in English history, full of conflict and change. Although its whereabouts remain a mystery, the fascination with this lost treasure continues to drive investigations and searches. Is it still buried in the marshes, waiting to be rediscovered, or was it looted and destroyed centuries ago? The answer, like the treasure itself, remains hidden, keeping the intrigue about this medieval enigma alive.

19.   The Treasure of the Caesars: Lost Riches of the Roman Empire

The Treasury of the Caesars refers to a mythical accumulation of wealth belonging to Roman emperors, which could include gold and silver coins, jewelry, statues, religious artifacts, and ceremonial objects. This treasure, according to legend, represented not only the material wealth of the Roman Empire, but also the power and magnificence of a civilization that dominated much of the ancient world.

Presumptive features:

Contents: Gold, silver, precious gems, religious objects, and art from the Roman era.

Original Location: It is believed to have been stored in the Imperial Palace in Rome and other strategic sites of the empire.

Beyond its material wealth, the treasure would be an invaluable window into the life, culture, and religion of the Roman Empire.

Over the centuries, Rome accumulated vast spoils of war, tributes from conquered provinces, and contributions from its citizens. Emperors such as Augustus and Trajan reinforced the empire's reputation as one of the wealthiest civilizations of antiquity. These treasures were stored in temples, fortresses, and underground chambers to protect them from looting.

With the crisis of the third century AD and the eventual fall of the Western Roman Empire in 476 AD, much of this wealth disappeared. Some believe that they were sacked by barbarian invaders such as the Visigoths, who took Rome in 410 AD, or the Vandals, who stormed it in 455 AD. Others maintain that the treasure was hidden by loyalists of the Empire to avoid capture.

The idea of a lost treasure of the Roman Empire has inspired historians, archaeologists, and adventurers for centuries. From early medieval explorers to modern research, the Treasure of the Caesars remains one of the greatest archaeological mysteries.

Many believe that the emperors hid the treasure in tunnels in Rome, such as the catacombs or the Cloaca Maxima sewer system. Some searches have identified sealed underground chambers that could hold part of the treasure.

Others think that, after the foundation of Constantinople by Constantine in the fourth century, a significant part of the imperial treasury was transferred there. This movement may have included the most valuable objects.

Since the Visigoths and Vandals sacked Rome on different occasions, some historians suggest that they took the treasure back to their respective territories, but there are no clear records of its fate.

According to one legend, a portion of the treasure was transported by ship and lost in a shipwreck in the Mediterranean.

It is also possible that some of the treasure was hidden in fortresses or outlying cities of the empire, such as Ravenna or Carthage, during the last days of Rome.

Interesting facts:

The Visigothic king Alaric died shortly after sacking Rome in 410 AD. According to legend, he was buried along with his share of the loot in a river near Cosenza, Italy. It is said that part of the Treasure of the Caesars could be in this tomb never found.

In recent years, archaeologists have explored tunnels beneath the Colosseum and Roman Forum in search of sealed chambers that could house remains of the treasure.

Some historians believe that the riches of the Temple of Capitoline Jupiter, a key part of the imperial treasury, may have been hidden before the fall of Rome.

Part of the imperial wealth transferred to Constantinople was plundered during the Fourth Crusade in 1204. However, no trace of the most important artifacts has been found.

The Treasury of the Caesars is a symbol of the splendor and decline of the Roman Empire, a testament to its power and, at the same time, a reflection of its vulnerability. Although fragments of this wealth have been found in archaeological excavations, most of it remains lost, shrouded in legends and uncertainties. Their search continues to captivate archaeologists and adventurers, who hope that one day the secrets of

Rome and its majestic treasure will be revealed. Are you in forgotten tunnels beneath the Eternal City, in the depths of the Mediterranean, or a remote corner of ancient Europe? The answer remains an enigma.

20.   Marie Antoinette's Necklace: Intrigue, Legend and Mystery

One of the most famous and controversial objects in history, Marie Antoinette's Necklace was an extraordinary piece of jewelry. Designed to dazzle, this necklace was a symbol of luxury and opulence at the court of France.

Necklace features: Among its materials are diamonds of the highest quality, set in gold and silver. Its design consisted of multiple rows of diamonds set in an elaborate structure that included a central pendant. At the time, its cost was estimated to be equivalent to millions of dollars today.

The necklace was commissioned by King Louis XV for his mistress, Madame du Barry. However, the monarch died before handing it over, leaving the jewel in the possession of jewelers Boehmer and Bassenge, who tried to sell it to other customers of the nobility.

Although Marie Antoinette did not desire the necklace, her name became attached to it due to the infamous Necklace Scandal. In 1785, a woman named Jeanne de la Motte-Valois devised an elaborate fraud to obtain the necklace, posing as the queen's intermediary. The deception involved fake letters and identity theft in clandestine meetings.

When the fraud was discovered, although Marie Antoinette had no direct connection to the case, her reputation suffered greatly. The scandal increased the discredit of the monarchy, contributing to the climate that led to the French Revolution.

The necklace was dismembered, and its diamonds were sold by Jeanne de la Motte-Valois and her accomplices. However, parts of the jewel may have survived, which has led to numerous searches and speculations over the centuries.

Some historians believe that the diamonds in the necklace were sold to different buyers, but they could have been used in the creation of other pieces of jewelry.

Another theory suggests that part of the necklace may have been hidden by Jeanne or her associates in an attempt to save themselves after the scandal.

Since Jeanne de la Motte-Valois fled to England, it is speculated that she sold some diamonds there to finance her life in exile.

It can also be assumed that some fragments could have made it onto the black market or private collections without their original provenance being recognized.

Interesting facts:

Although the necklace bears her name, the queen never wore it or showed interest in acquiring it. His link with the scandal was circumstantial.

The Necklace Scandal was one of the main causes of the French monarchy's loss of popularity, helping to fan the flames of the French Revolution.

Some fictional accounts suggest that a portion of the necklace could have been recovered and preserved by descendants of royalty, although there is no strong evidence to support this idea.

The necklace's history has inspired novels, films, and operas, cementing it as a symbol of intrigue and decadence.

Marie Antoinette's Necklace not only represents a jewel of extraordinary beauty but also a crucial chapter in the history of France, marked by deception, politics, and the consequences of a scandal that changed the course of history. Although fragments of this legendary object may have survived, its true legacy lies in the fascination it continues to generate and the role it played in the fall of a monarchy. Their exact whereabouts may remain a mystery, but their impact lingers in the collective imagination.

21.   The Golden Cross of the Battle of Bosworth: A Lost Symbol of English History

The Golden Cross of the Battle of Bosworth is a historical jewel linked to Richard III, the last king of the House of York. The cross, made of pure gold and decorated with precious gems, is said to have symbolized both the Christian faith and the authority of the monarch.

Characteristics of the Cross:

Materials: Solid gold, encrusted with rubies, emeralds, and sapphires.
Design: A Latin cross that included a reliquary, possibly with a small sacred relic.
Dimensions: Although its exact size is uncertain, it is described as large enough to be ostentatious in battle, carried on the king's royal standard or personal baggage.

The Battle of Bosworth (1485) marked the end of the Wars of the Roses, a dynastic conflict that pitted the houses of York and Lancaster against each other. Richard III was killed in the engagement, and his defeat meant Henry Tudor's rise as Henry VII, inaugurating the Tudor dynasty.

The cross, according to records, accompanied Richard III in battle, as part of his royal equipment and personal emblem.

Following the defeat and death of Richard III, his personal belongings, including the standard and cross, disappeared in the chaos that followed. It is presumed that it was taken as spoils of war by the victorious forces or stolen by battlefield looters.

The cross has been an object of fascination for historians and treasure hunters. Their trail is lost after the battle, and their whereabouts remain an enigma.

Some suggest that the cross was melted down shortly after the battle to take advantage of its material value. This was a common practice at the time, especially with gold objects.

Others believe that the cross may have been secretly buried near the battlefield, perhaps by soldiers who planned to retrieve it later.

It is also argued that Henry VII, in consolidating his power, may have claimed the cross as a symbol of victory, using it to legitimize his reign. However, there are no records to support this theory.

Some theorists speculate that the cross may have been sold to foreign merchants or even taken to another country, far from England.

The cross is said to have contained a sacred relic, possibly a fragment of the True Cross, which adds to its spiritual and historical value.

The cross is seen as an emblem of the tragic end of Richard III, whose figure has been the subject of debate and historical redemption following the discovery of his remains in 2012.

Archaeologists and treasure hunters have carried out explorations in the Bosworth area using advanced technology, but so far, the cross has not been located.

The Golden Cross of the Battle of Bosworth remains a symbol of a turbulent time in English history. Although his whereabouts remain unknown, his legacy lives on in the collective imagination as a reminder of the struggle for power and the mystery surrounding the precious objects of history. Their discovery, if it ever happens, would be a monumental find that would shed new light on one of the most decisive events of the English monarchy.

22. The Romanovs' Treasure: A Vanishing Fortune in the Revolution

The Romanov Treasure is one of the greatest enigmas in modern history. He is referring to the legendary fortune accumulated by the Romanov dynasty, which ruled Russia for more than three centuries until its overthrow in 1917. This treasure would include gold, jewelry, artwork, historical documents, and priceless objects.

Treasure Items: Includes tiaras, necklaces, rings, and brooches of the Tsars and Tsarinas, some decorated with diamonds, emeralds, and rubies of exceptional cut. Also, religious art: gold and silver icons, sacred chalices, and crosses encrusted with gems. Money and gold: Coins, gold bars, and other wealth of the State. Personal Heirlooms: These include personal items of the Romanov family, such as diaries, clothing, and utensils.

The Romanov dynasty accumulated unimaginable riches thanks to the vast Russian empire, which was rich in natural resources and precious minerals. These riches were kept in the Winter Palace in St. Petersburg and other royal residences.

With the abdication of Nicholas II in 1917 and the triumph of the Bolshevik Revolution, the Romanov family was arrested. In 1918, Nicholas II and his family were executed in Yekaterinburg. During this chaos, the whereabouts of their assets became uncertain.

The Bolsheviks confiscated much of the riches, but it is believed that a significant portion of the treasure disappeared before they arrived.

Since the 20th century, historians, treasure hunters, and adventurers have tried to locate the lost riches of the Romanovs. Theories about its location have led to searches in Siberia, St. Petersburg, and abroad.

A popular theory suggests that loyal followers of the Romanovs buried part of the treasure near the place where the family was executed.

Some believe that the treasure was sent abroad by allies of the Romanovs before the final fall of the dynasty. Europe, particularly Switzerland and France, is frequently mentioned as a possible destination.

Another hypothesis posits that much of the treasure was seized by the revolutionaries and later sold on international markets to finance the new Soviet government.

It is also likely that the treasure was scattered in small parts among looters, members of the Bolshevik regime, and art dealers, making it difficult to trace.

Interesting facts:

Some Romanov jewels have reappeared at international auctions, sold as anonymous treasures.

Declassified Bolshevik archives in the 1990s revealed partial inventories of the confiscated jewels, but not all of it is accounted for.

The scavenger hunt has inspired books, movies, and conspiracy theories, from the mystery of Princess Anastasia to connections to treasures in Europe.

The Romanov Treasury remains a symbol of the splendor and fall of a dynasty, a reflection of Russian might and the cost of revolutionary changes. While his exact whereabouts remain a mystery, his story continues to fascinate those who search in his glitter not only for wealth but also for the keys to a tumultuous past. If it is ever discovered, it could shed light on one of the most dramatic episodes in modern history.

23.   The Sword of Ali: A Lost Symbol of Islamic History

The Sword of Ali, also known as Zulfiqar, is one of the most famous and legendary weapons in Islamic history. The sword, which is attributed to the fourth caliph of Islam, Ali ibn Abi Talib, has great symbolic importance both religiously and historically. It is known for its distinctive double-blade design, which makes it unique among medieval weapons.

The Zulfiqar is famous for its forked blade, with two edges at the end, representing both strength and justice. This peculiar shape makes it a visual symbol of courage and honor.

Although details about its construction are uncertain, it is believed that the sword was made of high-quality steel, possibly the result of the metallurgical advances of the time.

The Zulfiqar was large enough to be used in both hand-to-hand combat and large-scale battles.

The Zulfiqar has its origins in the early days of Islam, particularly during the Battle of Uhud in 625 AD, where Ali ibn Abi Talib, cousin and son-in-law of the Prophet Muhammad, was appointed to carry the sword. During this battle, the sword gained a reputation due to Ali's bravery and skill in using it to defend his army and defeat enemies. He is credited with a series of victories and heroics that helped cement his image as a legendary warrior.

According to Islamic traditions, Muhammad gave the Zulfiqar to Ali as a symbol of divine power, and the sword became an emblem of justice and the struggle for good. Its use continued to be an important symbol in subsequent military campaigns led by Ali, who would later become the fourth caliph of Islam.

Ali's sword has been the subject of numerous legends and is said to have been passed down from generation to generation, but its exact whereabouts have been a mystery for centuries. There are several stories about what happened to the sword after the death of Ali and his successors.

One of the most widely accepted theories is that Zulfiqar was lost during the internal struggles of the caliphate, especially with the rise of the Abbasid caliphate in the eighth century. Many of the objects belonging to the early caliphs were looted, and the sword may have been lost in that period.

The sword is also said to have been in the city of Kufa (present-day Iraq), and some accounts claim that it was kept there for centuries, in the mosque that Ali founded. However, after the invasions and looting, the whereabouts of the sword are obscured.

Some historians suggest that the Zulfiqar may have come to Egypt, having been guarded by the Fatimid dynasty, which ruled in North Africa. This hypothesis is based on the well-known relationship between the Fatimids and Ali's lineage.

Another less verified theory holds that the Zulfiqar was kept secret within the caliph's descended families, the

Sayyids and that it remains somewhere in the Middle East, hidden from the authorities.

The Zulfiqar is a powerful emblem in Islam, especially in the context of the Shiite branch, where Ali and his sword are considered symbols of divine justice and sacrifice.

In some Islamic traditions, the Zulfiqar is seen as a sacred sword, an object of divine power that could appear in times of great need to protect believers from injustice.

The Zulfiqar has also been a powerful symbol in Islamic literature and art, being depicted in numerous art objects, such as sculptures, paintings, and tapestries.

The symbol of the Zulfiqar is used on the emblems and flags of various Shiite groups, especially those that identify with the figure of Ali and the struggle for justice.

The Sword of Ali, or Zulfiqar, is an emblem that transcends military history to become a religious and cultural symbol. Over the centuries, their whereabouts have become one of the great mysteries of Islamic history. Despite numerous theories, no conclusive evidence of its location has been found, which has only increased its mysticism and appeal. In any case, his legacy continues to be a powerful source of inspiration, representing the struggle for justice, courage, and the defense of divine principles.

24. The Holy Grail and the Ark of the Covenant: Christian Religious Relics

The Holy Grail is one of the most iconic and enigmatic objects in history, deeply associated with the legend of King Arthur and the quest of the Knights of the Round Table. It is primarily described as the chalice used by Jesus Christ during the Last Supper, and to which, according to Christian tradition, divine powers are attributed, including the ability to grant eternal life, cure disease, or even offer mystical visions of God. Over the centuries, it has been a symbol of purity, power, and access to the divine.

It is traditionally described as a chalice, a cup, or a vessel that could be made of gold, silver, crystal, or gemstones. Throughout history, it has represented the connection between the divine and the human, being an object of devotion and mysticism.

According to Christian tradition, the Holy Grail is the chalice that Jesus used to distribute wine during the Last Supper, which is the time when he instituted the Eucharist. Legend holds that Joseph of Arimathea was the disciple who collected the blood of Christ in this chalice during the crucifixion and took it to Britain, where it was kept secret.

The popularity of the Holy Grail was consolidated in the Middle Ages when Arthurian legends incorporated it into their stories. In medieval romances, especially in the writings of Chrétien de Troyes, the Grail becomes the central object of a sacred quest, in which knights, such as Lancelot, Perceval, and Gilead, seek to achieve salvation and redemption.

The Holy Grail is not directly mentioned in the canonical gospels, but it appears in the apocryphal texts and other esoteric traditions. In some mystical accounts, such as in Robert de Boron's Legend of the Grail, the chalice is linked to Christ's lineage, adding a dimension of real and spiritual inheritance to the object.

The search for the Holy Grail has been one of the most fascinating subjects in history, inspiring countless expeditions and explorations, both in medieval tradition and in modern times.

During the Middle Ages, the Knights of the Round Table, led by King Arthur, were the main seekers of the Grail. According to legend, his mission was to find the chalice and bring it back to Camelot, which would bring salvation to the kingdom and eternal prosperity.

It is speculated that the Templars may have found the Grail and kept it a secret. During the persecution and dissolution of the order by Pope Clement V in 1312, many of the Templars were arrested and tortured to reveal the location of the Grail.

Over the centuries, various theories have emerged about the location of the Holy Grail, based on legends, ancient texts, and speculations.

One theory suggests that the Grail is in Jerusalem, possibly on Mount Zion, linked to the early Christians or the followers of Joseph of Arimathea. Some believe that the Grail is kept in the Chapel of the Virgin, a sacred place in the church of the Dormition of the Virgin Mary.

Rosslyn Chapel, located in Scotland, has been a key place in modern theories about the Grail. This chapel, known for its architecture and for being linked to the Templar order, is mentioned in the Da Vinci Code as one of the possible resting places of the Grail.

According to some legends, the Holy Grail arrived in Spain in the eighth century, brought by the Visigoths or the Templars. In the Cathedral of Valencia, a cup is preserved that some believe could be the Holy Grail. This cup, known as The Chalice of the Supper, has been associated with the Grail in various traditions.

Others believe that the Grail was never a physical object, but represents a spiritual concept, accessible only to those who follow a path of purity and devotion. In this interpretation, the Grail could be hidden in a secret place, reserved only for the most worthy.

The legend of the Holy Grail has inspired many literary and cinematographic works, such as Indiana Jones and The Last Crusade, where the Grail is presented as a source of immortality.

Although there is no concrete evidence of its existence, the Grail has been a symbol of Christian devotion, related to the blood of Christ and salvation.

The fascination with the Grail and its link with the Templars has given rise to numerous theories about the concealment of mystical secrets, as in the case of the novel The Da Vinci Code by Dan Brown.

Some theories hold that the Holy Grail is related to the lineage of Christ, especially royal descent, which has given rise to theories about the "descendants of Jesus."

The Holy Grail remains one of the great mysteries of history, an object of fervent devotion, exploration, and speculation. Whether as a symbol of immortality, divinity, or justice, its pursuit continues to captivate humanity. Whether the Grail is found in a church, on a distant mountain, or in some corner of the human soul, its legacy endures as a beacon of hope, faith, and mystery.

Nature of the Ark of the Covenant

The Ark of the Covenant is one of the most sacred and mysterious objects in ancient history. According to the Bible, the Ark was a wooden box covered with gold, designed to contain the tablets of the Law that Moses received from God at Mount Sinai. In addition to the tablets, the Ark is believed to have housed other sacred objects, such as the manna that fed the Israelites during their journey through the desert and the rod of Aaron, Moses' brother, which flourished as a sign of divine election.

The Ark was considered the very manifestation of God's presence on Earth, and according to the scriptures, it possessed extraordinary divine powers. It was said that whoever touched it without due respect or in inappropriate circumstances, suffered severe punishments. In Jewish and Christian tradition, the

Ark is a symbol of the covenant between God and his people.

According to the Bible, the Ark of the Covenant was built under God's direct instructions, during the exodus of the Israelites from Egypt. The design, which is described in the Book of Exodus, specifies that the Ark was to be made of acacia wood and covered with pure gold, both inside and outside. At the top of the Ark, there was a "mercy seat", a golden lid on which were placed two cherubs, angelic figures that symbolized the presence of God.

The Ark was kept in the Tabernacle, the portable sanctuary that accompanied the Israelites on their journey through the wilderness. Later, when the Israelites established their kingdom in the Promised Land, the Ark was placed in Solomon's Temple in Jerusalem, where it became the central object of worship.

The fate of the Ark of the Covenant following the destruction of the First Temple in Jerusalem in 586 B.C. has been the subject of debate and mystery for centuries. When the Babylonians destroyed the Temple, it is not known for certain whether they took the Ark or whether it was hidden by the Israelite priests before the invasion. From that moment on, the Ark disappears completely from historical records.

There are several theories about its disappearance, from that it was taken to Babylon and lost in subsequent invasions, to the possibility that it was hidden in some secret place in Jerusalem or even taken to distant lands by the priests.

For centuries, the Ark of the Covenant has been the object of fascination and mystery. Her disappearance has generated numerous searches and expeditions to locate her, but to date, no concrete trace has been found.

Since the Middle Ages, many expeditions and searches have been made to find it. During the 19th century, archaeologists and adventurers began to explore the region of Jerusalem and its surroundings in search of any hint of its location. Despite the efforts, no trace was found to confirm the existence of the sacred object.

In more recent times, searches for the Ark of the Covenant have intensified, with archaeologists, researchers, and even treasure hunters conducting explorations in various geographic locations. One of the most popular theories is that the Ark is located in Ethiopia, specifically in the church of St. Mary of Zion in Axum. Followers of this theory maintain that the Ark was brought there by King Menelik I, who, according to tradition, was the son of the Queen of Sheba and King Solomon. According to this legend, Menelik would have taken the Ark to Ethiopia to preserve and protect it.

Another hypothesis suggests that the Ark of the Covenant is hidden in a secret location within Jerusalem. Some believe it was hidden in a tunnel or chamber under the Temple Mount, the site where the Ark was originally located in Solomon's Temple. Excavations in the area have been limited due to the political and religious sensitivity of the area, which has fueled speculation about the Ark's possible location.

Another possibility is that the Ark was destroyed or lost during the Babylonian invasion in 586 B.C. In the absence of concrete evidence of its fate, some historians argue that the Ark may have been stripped or destroyed during the fall of Jerusalem.

Some ancient historians suggested that the Ark was brought to Rome or Constantinople during the Roman Empire or Byzantine Empire. According to this theory, the Ark would have been transferred to the capital of the empire for protection.

Interesting facts:

The Ark of the Covenant has been a source of inspiration in popular culture. Its most famous modern depiction is in the film Indiana Jones and the Raiders of the Lost Ark (1981), in which the main archaeologist, Indiana Jones, searches for the Ark before the Nazis can seize it.

According to the Bible, the Ark not only served as a receptacle for the Tablets of the Law but was also an object of power, capable of performing miracles. It is said that the Ark could open the sea, destroy walls, and even defeat entire armies.

The Temple Mount in Jerusalem, where the Ark was located, is one of the holiest places in the world for Judaism, Christianity, and Islam. Currently, the site is home to the Dome of the Rock and the Al-Aqsa Mosque, two of the most important places for Muslims.

The Ark of the Covenant remains one of the greatest mysteries in history. Despite efforts and theories about its location, its whereabouts remain uncertain. Whether it rests in Ethiopia, hidden in the bowels of Jerusalem, or was destroyed in ancient times, the Ark remains a powerful symbol of faith, mystery, and the human search for the divine.

25.   The Treasure of San Juan Island: Myth, History and Mystery

The treasure of San Juan Island is one of the most enigmatic and fascinating treasures in history. This treasure is believed to have been hidden by pirates on the island of San Juan, located in the Caribbean, off the coast of Puerto Rico. According to legends, the treasure would consist of large quantities of gold, silver, jewels, and priceless objects, which would have been looted from Spanish ships and other ships during the golden age of piracy in the seventeenth century. The mystery about the exact location of the treasure has captivated explorers, treasure hunters, and curious onlookers for centuries.

The history of the treasure of San Juan Island dates to the period of great pirate activity in the Caribbean when buccaneers and corsairs operated in waters near the Spanish colonies. It is said that, in 1671, the famous pirate Henry Morgan, known for his raids in the Americas, plundered several Spanish ships and accumulated immense booty.

After their looting, Morgan and other pirates would have decided to hide their treasure on an uninhabited island, to prevent the ships of the Spanish fleet from tracking the loot. It is believed that they chose the Island of San Juan due to its strategic location and its accessibility from different points in the Caribbean.

The small island became a haven for pirates looking to hide their wealth or escape from authorities. During the decades of piracy in the Caribbean, it is estimated that thousands of tons of gold and silver were looted from Spanish ships, and some of this treasure may have been lost on the island.

Historical accounts also mention that Morgan's booty consisted of gold bars, jewelry, and other precious objects that pirates had taken from Spanish trade routes. It is believed that, after hiding it, some of the pirates who knew its location died or were captured, taking the secret of the treasure to the grave.

The San Juan Island Treasure Hunt has been a recurring theme over the centuries, with explorers and treasure hunters attempting to discover its whereabouts. However, due to the lack of evidence and the numerous legends surrounding the story, the exact location of the treasure remains a mystery.

Since the 18th century, explorers have visited the island in search of the legendary treasure, with some claiming to have found clues pointing to its location. However, expeditions have not been successful in unearthing vast amounts of wealth. Legends have helped fuel the fascination with the treasure, with stories telling of mysterious symbols, hidden maps, and traces of gold on the ground.

One of the main challenges of the search is that it is not known for sure if the treasure is still on the island, or if it ever existed on the scale that legends suggest. The island, although small, has dense vegetation and rugged terrain, which has made searches difficult.

One of the most intriguing stories about the treasure of San Juan Island is that, after hiding the loot, the pirates tasked with protecting it died or mysteriously disappeared, leaving the treasure forgotten. It is speculated that the place where he was hidden could have been altered by natural changes, such as hurricanes, landslides, or volcanic eruptions.

One of the most common theories is that the treasure is hidden in the island's underground caverns, which pirates use as a shelter. These caverns, which are difficult to access, could have served as a safe hiding place for treasure. However, expeditions have found little evidence in the caves, making this theory more of a myth than a certainty.

Another hypothesis points out that the treasure could have been hidden underwater, near the coast, to prevent it from being discovered by the Spanish. Over the centuries, fluctuations in sea level could have submerged the treasure or scattered its remains on the seafloor. This has led to several underwater expeditions, but so far no conclusive evidence has been found.

Others believe that the treasure lies hidden among the island's dense forests and hills. In these areas, it is held that pirates buried the riches, ensuring that only those with the right map could access it. Accounts of location signs and symbols are still debated among treasure hunters.

Interesting facts:

The island is located in the Caribbean, off the coast of Puerto Rico, and has a rich history related to piracy. Over the centuries, it was used as a refuge by numerous pirates, including Henry Morgan and Jean Lafitte.

Morgan was one of the most notorious pirates of the time, known for his attacks on Spanish settlers in the Caribbean. Although it is known that she accumulated great wealth, there is no concrete evidence that any of them were buried on the Island of San Juan.

Despite modern attempts to find the treasure, underwater searches have not produced great results. On several occasions, small valuables have been found, but the full treasure has never been discovered.

The treasure of San Juan Island remains one of the most attractive mysteries in the Caribbean. Its existence and location continue to fuel the dream of finding lost wealth, which could reveal secrets of piracy and plunder on the seas of the seventeenth century. Although no conclusive evidence has been found about its whereabouts, the history and legends surrounding this treasure continue to captivate explorers and adventurers who dream of discovering what could be one of the greatest treasures ever found.

26.   The Treasure of the Golden Dolphins: Myth, History and Mystery

The Golden Dolphin Treasure is a legend that has fascinated generations of treasure hunters, adventurers, and historians. It is believed that this treasure, composed of an immense amount of gold and jewels, was left on Pearl Island, in the Gulf of Panama, by an ancient civilization that worshipped dolphins as sacred figures. The name "Golden Dolphins" refers to the incredible wealth that the island was said to possess, with gold objects and religious ornaments in the shape of dolphins, some of which would have been brought from South America and others from the Pacific islands.

The legend of the Golden Dolphin treasure is shrouded in mystery and is a mixture of pre-Columbian myths and historical accounts. The civilization that inhabited the region before the arrival of the European conquerors is believed to have been an advanced society that revered dolphins, sea creatures regarded as messengers of the gods. This civilization, although not identified with certainty, was known for its riches, which were jealously guarded in hidden temples on Pearl Island, in Panama.

According to legend, the inhabitants of the island made statues and ritual objects in the shape of dolphins, using gold and precious metals. These treasures were hidden in secret places by civilization fearing the arrival of the Spanish conquistadors, who plundered and destroyed indigenous peoples in search of riches.

The arrival of the Spanish conquistadors, led by Francisco Pizarro in the sixteenth century, forever altered the destiny of the indigenous civilizations of the region. Although the Spanish did not find the Golden Dolphin Treasure, stories about the island's riches circulated among the conquistadors and explorers of the time. Accounts mentioned large amounts of gold, temples hidden deep within the island, and religious symbols of golden dolphins.

In some accounts, it is described how the natives, when attacked by the Spanish, hid their treasures in secret places, knowing that the invaders would destroy their temples and take with them everything they could find.

Over the centuries, the treasure of Golden Dolphins has captivated numerous explorers, treasure hunters, and adventurers. Pearl Island, where the treasure is believed to have been buried, has been the subject of numerous expeditions, but no conclusive trace of the treasure has been found so far.

The first expeditions to the island began in the 17th century when tales of lost gold became popular among Spanish and Portuguese treasure hunters. However, the island is small and its terrain rugged, making searches in the region tricky. Over the centuries, numerous expeditions were made without success, and the island was shrouded in more mystery than ever.

In 1920, one of the most notable expeditions was organized by a group of American and European adventurers, who believed that the treasure might be buried somewhere in the interior of the island. Using primitive tools and maps from the colonial era, explorers searched the mountains and coastal areas finding nothing but remains of ancient structures that might have belonged to indigenous peoples.

The lack of success in these searches, coupled with the disappearance of historical records that could have indicated the exact location of the treasure, left many with the feeling that the Golden Dolphin treasure might just be a legend.

One of the most widely accepted theories is that the treasure was submerged in the sea by the island's natives to protect it from invaders. It is speculated that the ancient guardians of the treasure would have thrown it into the ocean, using the coral reefs and deep waters as hiding places. This has led to underwater expeditions in search of gold artifacts and ritual objects.

Others believe that the treasure was hidden in some hidden cave within the island, a place accessible only by complicated and secret paths. Over the years, some explorers have claimed to have found hints of underground entrances to the island, but none of these theories have been confirmed.

Some treasure hunters claim that the treasure is buried under the sands or in some corner of the island that has not yet been thoroughly explored. According to some accounts, the natives would have used symbols to indicate the location of the treasure, but these codes were lost over time.

Interesting facts:

Panama's Pearl Island is known for its pearl-rich waters and history as a trading location. Over the centuries, the island has been a hub of activity for pirates, traders, and colonizers.

In several pre-Columbian cultures of the Caribbean and South America, dolphins were considered sacred animals, associated with gods and protective spirits of the sea. This fueled the legend that golden dolphins were symbols of power and wealth.

As piracy declined in the Caribbean, many of the legends about lost treasures, including those of the Golden Dolphins, became part of regional folklore, fueling myths and fables that still endure.

The treasure of the Golden Dolphins remains one of the greatest mysteries in the history of piracy in the Caribbean. Despite the efforts of explorers and treasure hunters for centuries, the treasure remains missing, shrouded in myths, speculations, and legends. As technology improves, the search continues, but the exact location of the treasure remains hidden, leaving dreamers hoping that one day, in some corner of the island or the depths of the sea, the secrets of this fabulous treasure will be revealed.

27.   The Chalice of Doña Urraca: History, mystery and search for a lost treasure

The Chalice of Doña Urraca is a legendary object that has been the object of fascination and mystery for centuries. It is a chalice of great value, both material and symbolic, which is associated with Queen Urraca de León, an important figure in the medieval history of the Iberian Peninsula. This chalice, although it has been lost in time, is described as a sacred cup of gold, encrusted with precious stones, and with a history full of religious symbolism and political power.

According to tradition, the Chalice of Doña Urraca was not only an object of veneration but also a symbol of the legitimacy and power of the queen. It was said that the chalice had been used in important moments of the Leonese monarchy and that it had a much greater meaning than its material value since it represented the connection between divine power and the throne of León.

Doña Urraca was a queen of the Crown of León in the eleventh century, born in 1081, daughter of King Alfonso VI of León and Castile. Urraca stood out not only for his intelligence and political ambition but also for the dynastic conflicts that marked his reign. She was a woman who fought to maintain control of her territories amid a tumultuous time, marked by disputes between different noble factions and rivalry with her ex-husband, Alfonso I of Aragon, with whom she had a relationship marked by power struggles.

The Chalice of Doña Urraca is associated with the queen due to the tradition that states that she possessed it as a symbol of authority and legitimacy. The story goes that, in a symbolic act of her power, Doña Urraca used the chalice during an important religious ceremony, which reinforced her image as a divine monarch backed by the Church.

The Chalice of Doña Urraca disappeared from historical records as time progressed. During her reign, there is no clear evidence that the chalice was given or stolen, but it is believed that it was preserved at the Leonese court after the queen died in 1111. Its whereabouts began to become uncertain after the fall of León as a center of power and the political reconfiguration of the region.

Some legends suggest that, after Urraca's death, the chalice was taken as booty during the invasions or conflicts that shook the region, while others suggest that it was hidden to preserve its symbolic and material value.

Since the Middle Ages, rumors about the location of the chalice have not ceased. Neighboring kingdoms, such as those of Castile and Aragon, were involved in constant conflicts for control of the territories of León, which may have influenced the fate of the chalice. Some historians have suggested that, in times of instability, the chalice may have been taken out of León to prevent it from falling into enemy hands.

In modern times, some research and even excavations have been carried out in places related to Queen Urraca and the Kingdom of León. However, none of these expeditions have been successful in locating the chalice, which has added to the mystery surrounding its whereabouts.

One of the oldest hypotheses suggests that the chalice was hidden in a church or monastery in the region of León or Salamanca. According to this theory, the chalice may have been preserved by the Church to prevent it from falling into the hands of invaders. Some believe that the chalice could be in a hidden place inside the historic churches of the region, where it has been kept for centuries.

Another hypothesis points to the catacombs of Toledo, a city with a rich Christian and historical tradition. This theory holds that the chalice may have been transported to Toledo during the time of the Reconquista to prevent its destruction or looting. It is believed that, under the protection of religious authorities, the chalice would have been hidden in some secret crypt or catacomb.

Given the tradition of hiding treasures in inaccessible places, some believe that the Chalice of Doña Urraca was taken to the mountains near León, where it could have been hidden for protection. The vast and rugged mountains of the region would have offered the perfect place to hide such a valuable and symbolic object.

Others argue that the chalice was taken abroad, perhaps to a safer place, outside the Iberian Peninsula, by those who wished to protect it from plunder. This theory suggests that the chalice may have been transported to lands beyond Europe, and today it could be in a museum or private collection somewhere unknown.

Interesting facts:

The Chalice of Doña Urraca not only had great material value due to its composition of gold and precious stones, but its symbolic value was even greater. It represented the queen's authority and the legitimacy of her reign, making it a sacred object of great power.

Doña Urraca lived in a time of great political instability. Her reign was marked by internal strife and wars against her ex-husband Alfonso I of Aragon, which caused a climate of tension and division in the Christian kingdoms of the Iberian Peninsula.

Although many have tried to find the chalice, to date no physical trace has been found to confirm its existence or current whereabouts. The Chalice of Doña Urraca remains a mystery that attracts archaeologists and treasure hunters alike.

The Chalice of Doña Urraca is an object of great historical and religious importance, whose whereabouts remain unknown. Over the centuries, their search has given rise to numerous theories, from their possible concealment in the churches of León to their disappearance in distant lands. However, the chalice remains one of the great mysteries of medieval history, a lost treasure that has captured the imagination of generations of relic seekers and adventurers.

28. Napoleon's Sword: A Symbol of Power and Mystery

Napoleon's Sword is one of the most coveted and enigmatic historical objects in military history. This sword, which belonged to the French Emperor Napoleon Bonaparte, is a symbol of his power and ambition during the Napoleonic Wars. It is considered an object not only of material value, but also of great historical and cultural significance, representing the rise and fall of one of the most influential leaders in history.

The sword that is known as the "Napoleon's Sword" is not a single sword, but several, as Napoleon possessed different swords throughout his life. However, the most famous and most sought after is the sword of honor that was given to him in 1804, when he was crowned Emperor of France. The sword is famous for its elegance, its symbolism, and the fact that it was used at key moments in his reign.

The sword is typically French, with a gold hilt and an elegant pommel bearing the inscription "Napoléon Bonaparte, Empereur des Français". The blade is made of steel and decorated with intricate details symbolizing Napoleon's strength and majesty.

More than its materiality, the sword is a symbol of Napoleon's ambition, who used it at decisive moments in his career, such as in the battles of Austerlitz and Wagram.

Napoleon Bonaparte, who rose to power during the French Revolution, proclaimed himself emperor of

France in 1804, establishing the First French Empire. During his reign, Napoleon fought a series of wars, known as the Napoleonic Wars, which involved several European nations. In these conflicts, Napoleon sought to expand his empire, coming to dominate much of Europe.

The sword given to Napoleon in 1804 was a gift from the French government, symbolizing recognition of his ascension to the imperial throne. The sword, which was not only a weapon but also an emblem of his authority, was decorated with elements that represented the glory of the French Empire. Throughout his reign, Napoleon used several swords for different occasions, but the one in 1804 was the most representative of his power.

After Napoleon's defeat at the Battle of Waterloo in 1815 and his subsequent exile to the island of St. Helena, many of the symbols of his empire, including his personal belongings, were dispersed. During this time, Napoleon's sword was lost to sight, and its whereabouts became a mystery.

Over the years, its search has fascinated collectors, historians, and adventurers. The sword has become a highly coveted object, not only because of its material value but also because of its historical significance.

After Napoleon's defeat, some of his assets were confiscated and distributed among the victorious European powers. It is known that one of his swords was given to the British royal family, but it is not certain whether the 1804 sword of honor was part of this delivery. Historical documents indicate that several swords, including the most famous, were lost in the looting and scattering of their belongings.

In the 20th and 21st centuries, historians and archaeologists have attempted to trace the whereabouts of the sword. Several museums have claimed to have swords related to Napoleon in their possession, but there is no consensus on which of them is the one that truly belonged to the emperor. In addition, international auctions have offered swords and other objects of Napoleon, some of which have been disputed by experts, since there is not always reliable documentation of their authenticity.

In 2015, a sword that allegedly belonged to Napoleon was sold at auction in France for more than 200,000 euros, although it has not been proven that it is the sword that was used in his coronation.

It is believed that some of Napoleon's swords were given to private collectors or European museums, such as the Army Museum in Paris or the Museum of Military History in Vienna. However, it has never been confirmed that the famous coronation sword is in the possession of any of these institutions.

The sword may be in the hands of a private collector, out of the reach of the public. Collectors of historical memorabilia have acquired several Napoleon-related pieces in the past, leaving open the possibility that the sword was sold on the black market or at a private auction.

Another theory holds that the sword was hidden after Napoleon's fall, perhaps by loyal members of his court or relatives. It is possible that, due to its symbolic value, the sword was kept to prevent its confiscation by the defeating powers.

After Napoleon's exile to the island of St. Helena, several of the emperor's personal belongings were sent to Russia, as part of the tsars' victory over the Napoleonic empire. Some suggest that the sword could have remained on Russian territory, although there is no clear documentary evidence.

The sword has appeared in numerous works of fiction, films, and books, where it is presented as an object of mystical power or a symbol of the greatness of the Napoleonic empire.

The value of the sword lies not only in the materials with which it was manufactured but also in the enormous symbolism it contains. It represents Napoleon's ambition and the collapse of his empire.

Napoleon's Sword remains an object shrouded in mystery and desire. Despite the efforts of historians and collectors to locate it, its whereabouts remain unsolved. However, the symbolism behind the sword, and its connection to the rise and fall of one of history's most influential emperors, continues to captivate the imagination of those who study Napoleon Bonaparte's legacy.

29.   The Blue Diamond of Tavernier: Mystery and Fascination

The Blue Diamond of Tavernier, also known as the "Blue Diamond", is one of the most famous and enigmatic treasures in the history of jewelry. This deep blue diamond stands out not only for its beauty but for its mysterious history, full of thieves, tragedies, and legends. Rectangular in cut and deep blue color, this diamond has captured the imagination of historians, jewelers, and collectors over the centuries.

It is a deep blue diamond, probably due to the presence of boron in its crystal structure. It is estimated that the original Blue Diamond weighed around 112 carats. The stone had a rudimentary carving, rectangular or "shield" shape, which allowed its color and brilliance to be highly appreciated.

The diamond was described as one of the largest and most beautiful ever discovered, with a history that is intertwined with the most important figures of European royalty and aristocracy. But its legend is also marked by a series of dark events, including a curse that seems to have accompanied the diamond throughout its life.

The Tavernier Blue Diamond was discovered in India, at the Kollur mine in the Golconda region, known for being the source of some of the world's most famous diamonds. It was found in the 17th century and is said to have been acquired by the French merchant Jean-Baptiste Tavernier, who brought it to Europe. Tavernier was a renowned merchant and traveler, famous for his expeditions in search of rare and exotic jewelry.

In 1668, Tavernier sold the diamond to King Louis XIV of France, known as the "Sun King," for an astronomical sum of 220,000 pounds. From this moment on, the diamond became part of the French royal collection.

After its acquisition by King Louis XIV, the Blue Diamond was mounted on a kind of brooch that adorned its clothing, known as the "Heart of Louis XIV". For years, the diamond was displayed as a symbol of the power and wealth of the French monarchy, being part of the rejoicing and pomp of the court.

However, the diamond's story was shrouded in tragedies and mysterious coincidences, fueling the legend that it was cursed. Over the years, several tragic events occurred in the French royal family, contributing to the belief that the diamond brought with it a fatal curse.

The curse associated with the Blue Diamond of Tavernier is one of the most intriguing legends surrounding this famous treasure. After the death of Louis XIV, the diamond passed into the hands of his great-grandson, Louis XV, who placed it in the royal crown. Over the years, the diamond seems to have brought with it a series of deaths and misfortunes to its owners.

The most well-known story of the diamond curse has to do with the death of Louis XV, who, like his predecessor, died under grim circumstances. In 1792, the French Revolution brought about the fall of the monarchy, and the diamond was stolen from the Palace of Versailles, along with other royal treasures. During this period of chaos, the Blue Diamond disappeared from the historical record.

Some historians believe that the curse continued to affect those who were related to the diamond, as the French Revolution led to the execution of several members of the royal family, including King Louis XVI and his wife, Marie Antoinette, who was also related to the diamond through the jewel of the "Marie Antoinette Necklace", Another famous historical incident, of which we have already related.

After the Blue Diamond was stolen in 1792, its whereabouts became a mystery. Despite the efforts of police and historians to track its fate, the diamond disappeared without a trace.

Some believe that the diamond was destroyed or lost in the tumultuous circumstances of the French Revolution, while others maintain that it was stolen by thieves who then sold or hid it. Throughout the nineteenth century, there were several attempts to locate it, but without success.

In 1812, it is believed that the diamond reappeared in the hands of a jeweler named Simon de Latorre, who sold it to a British merchant. In the 1830s, the diamond was acquired by a British jewelry collector who mounted it on a ring. However, in 1839, the diamond was again stolen and lost.

In 1851, it appeared at auction in London under the name "Blue Diamond", but it was not the same diamond as Tavernier's, as some experts claim that the diamond in question was a counterfeit version.

To this day, the exact whereabouts of the Blue Diamond of Tavernier remain one of the great mysteries. There are several hypotheses as to where it could be found:

Many believe that the diamond was destroyed or irreparably damaged during the riots of the French Revolution. It may have been melted down, altered, or lost forever.

Some suggest that the diamond was acquired by a private collector, who might have hidden it to avoid identification or recognition. This collector could have owned it for generations, keeping it off the public radar.

The most romantic hypothesis holds that the diamond is still hidden somewhere in France, perhaps buried or lost in the rubble of the Revolution. Some adventurers have searched for the jewel in the places where it was known to have been stolen, but so far they have not been successful.

Interesting facts:

It is believed that the Tavernier Blue Diamond could have been the precursor to the famous Hope Diamond, one of the most famous diamonds in the world, which also has a history of robberies and tragedies. Some suggest that both diamonds could have been related due to their similar characteristics.

Over the years, many people have considered the Tavernier Blue Diamond to be the "cursed jewel" for its ability to bring tragedy and suffering to its owners.

A similar example was auctioned in London in 1839, but it has never been proven to be Tavernier's original Blue Diamond.

The Tavernier Blue Diamond remains one of the most fascinating mysteries in historical jewelry. With a history spanning centuries of conquests, thefts, tragedies, and legends, his whereabouts remain uncertain. Whether it's in the hands of a private collector, hidden in the folds of history, or even lost forever, its name and history live on in the fascination it sparks in treasure hunters and those who are drawn to the mystery and danger surrounding the world's most valuable objects.

30. The Nazi Gold Train: Myth, Reality and Mystery

The "Nazi Gold Train" is one of the most intriguing and mysterious treasures in modern history. It is a train convoy that allegedly transported gold, jewelry, art, and other valuable objects stolen by the Nazi regime during World War II. This train would be hidden somewhere in Poland, near the city of Walbrzych, in the southwest of the country, specifically in the region of Lower Silesia.

The train is related to the last days of World War II, when the Nazi army, in its flight before the advance of the Allied forces, would have hidden this train loaded with treasures in a tunnel, according to various legends. The train is described as a kind of "mobile fortress" loaded with loot looted by the Nazis, which included gold, silver bars, weapons, and artwork stolen from museums and private collections.

Over the years, this train has become part of the mythology of the "lost treasure", fueling speculation and tireless searches.

During the Nazi occupation of Europe, the German war machine systematically plundered the resources and wealth of the invaded countries. Among the most valuable treasures the Nazis tried to seize were gold, jewelry, and works of art that had been stolen from banks, museums, and families of the European aristocracy. It is estimated that much of this loot was used to finance the war and the personal enrichment of the Nazi regime's top brass.

At the end of the war, with the fall of Berlin in 1945 and the advance of Soviet and Allied forces, the Nazis, fearful of the recovery of these treasures, decided to hide them in secret places. The train with stolen gold and art is said to have departed from Breslau (present-day Wroclaw, Poland) in the last period of the war, transporting a large amount of wealth to an unknown destination.

The legend of the Nazi Gold Train originated when several witnesses began claiming to have seen a train loaded with valuable objects during the last phase of the war. According to the most popular versions, the train was hidden in a network of secret tunnels in the Sudeten Mountains, a mountain range in the region of Silesia, present-day Poland. The theory held that the train was hidden in a system of tunnels dug by the Nazis to protect their riches.

After the war, many people claimed to have found clues to the train's location, but its exact whereabouts could never be confirmed. For years, the legend remained alive, without concrete evidence, fueled by rumors and testimonies of those who claimed to have seen the train or to have witnessed its concealment.

Over the years, various groups of treasure hunters attempted to locate the Nazi Gold Train in the Lower Silesia region, but without success. The lack of concrete evidence about its existence left researchers and treasure hunters facing the question: is this train a myth or does it exist?

Interest in the train was revived in 1990, when a couple of people claimed to have located the supposed tunnel in which the train was located, near Walbrzych. However, the Polish government did not allow any excavations without definitive evidence, leaving the search in the realm of speculation.

The search for the Nazi Gold Train gained new momentum in 2015, when two Polish treasure hunters, Andreas Richter, and Piotr Koper, claimed to have found the train in the town of Walbrzych, thanks to information they had gathered over years of research. Using advanced technology, such as ground-penetrating radar, the two men presented evidence that there was an underground object in the area that could be the train.

The discovery was confirmed by local authorities, and the Polish government stepped in to investigate the find. In 2016, the government authorized excavations in the area, but to date, the train has not been found, although geophysical studies continue. Efforts to excavate the area and recover the train have been complicated by difficult geography and the lack of definitive evidence.

There are several theories about the whereabouts of the Nazi Gold Train, although none have been conclusively proven. Some of the most common include:

Many experts believe that the train was hidden in a series of tunnels built by the Nazis in the Silesia region. These tunnels were designed to protect factories and warehouses from Allied bombing, so it would be logical for one of these locations to be used to hide a train full of riches.

Some historians suggest that while the train may have been initially hidden, the treasures were looted or destroyed before they could be found. Others claim that the train may have disintegrated over time due to environmental conditions or the passage of time.

There is a theory that the gold and valuables were removed from the train before it was hidden, scattering to various nearby locations. According to this theory, the train would not be the only hiding place for the treasure, several methods were used to hide it.

Despite searches and theories about its existence, the Nazi Gold Train remains a mystery. The lack of definitive proof of its whereabouts means that many still consider this treasure a legend.

If the train exists and is found, it is estimated that the value of the objects on board could be multimillions. In addition to gold, it is believed that it was carrying looted art and other valuable jewelry.

The Nazi Gold Train remains one of the great mysteries of World War II. Despite technological advances and new searches, the train has never been found conclusively. The story of this train and its lost treasure continues to fuel the fascination with the secrets of the past and the desire to discover what was hidden in the shadows of history. Meanwhile, the legend of the Nazi Gold Train continues to be an enigma that continues to be sought after by treasure hunters and experts in the history of war.

31. The Robbery at the Isabella Stewart Gardner Museum in Boston

The robbery at the Isabella Stewart Gardner Museum, one of the largest and most enigmatic in the history of art, occurred in the early morning of March 18, 1990. On that night, two men dressed as police officers entered the Boston Museum with an excuse: to investigate an incident involving a car parked without permission at the entrance. The security guards, complying with security protocols, allowed him to enter.

Once inside, the fake police officers took the guards hostage and asked them to open the museum's security cameras for them. Throughout the night, the thieves stole 13 pieces of art, belonging to some of the most renowned artists in history, such as Vermeer, Rembrandt, and Degas. The robbery was carried out with astonishing precision and without a single bullet being fired, leaving the museum in ruins and generating a mystery that persists to this day.

The pieces stolen in this theft are some of the most valuable and coveted in the art world. These are the works that disappeared that night:

"The Concert" by Johannes Vermeer: One of Vermeer's most famous paintings, depicting two women and a man playing music, was stolen. This work is considered one of the most valuable in the history of art.

Rembrandt's "The Storm on the Sea of Galilee": One of Rembrandt's most famous paintings, depicting a dramatic scene of a shipwreck at sea, was also stolen. This work has been one of the most sought-after.

"The Landscape with the Man Playing Cards" by Edgar Degas: This drawing by Degas was also stolen and is part of the works that disappeared that night.

"The Potty" by Francisco de Goya: An oil painting by Goya that disappeared in the robbery.

In addition to the works of Vermeer, Rembrandt, and Degas, pieces by artists such as Edouard Manet, Henri Matisse, and others were also stolen.

The total value of the stolen works is estimated to be around $500 million, making this theft one of the largest in art history. The stolen pieces are unique not only for their economic value but also for their historical and cultural significance.

For decades, theories about the whereabouts of stolen works have been numerous and varied. Some of the most accepted include:

One of the most popular theories is that the works were sold on the black market for art. It is believed that the stolen pieces were distributed to private collectors or art trafficking groups, who, being aware of the scale of the theft, kept them hidden.

Another hypothesis holds that the thieves destroyed or damaged the works to prevent them from being tracked. This could have occurred in an attempt to eliminate any traces that could lead to those responsible.

Some investigators have suggested that the robbery could have been linked to organized crime. The precision with which the thieves carried out the theft and the lack of clues as to their whereabouts suggest that the works could have been hidden to be sold or used as part of some illegal deal.

Another theory points to the Irish mafia, which influenced in the region at the time. It is believed that some members of the mafia may have had information about the stolen artworks, but no direct link has ever been confirmed.

Despite these various theories, none have been confirmed. The works are still missing, and the mystery persists.

The Isabella Stewart Gardner Museum, along with local and federal authorities, continues to search for the stolen works. In 2017, the museum increased the reward for information on the whereabouts of the pieces to $10 million, one of the largest rewards offered for stolen art in history.

The FBI, which has been involved in the investigation since the robbery, remains the lead agency tasked with solving the case. In 2013, the investigative agency said it knew the identity of the thieves but did not have enough evidence to bring them to justice. Still, solving the case remains a high-profile goal for authorities.

In a bid to restore the stolen pieces, the museum keeps a promise to return the works to their original place if they are ever recovered, no matter what condition they are in.

Robbery is the subject of several books, documentaries, and television shows: Robbery has inspired several investigations, documentaries, and even movies, including an episode of the famous Netflix series, Unsolved Mysteries.

The Isabella Stewart Gardner Museum still keeps a copy of the stolen pieces: To preserve the memory of the stolen works, the museum kept a reproduction of the paintings that disappeared, allowing visitors to see what was once there.

The robbery at the Isabella Stewart Gardner Museum remains one of the most shocking and intricate cases in the art world. Despite advances in investigations and numerous theories revolving around the whereabouts of the stolen works, the mystery persists. The theft of the masterpieces was not only a blow to the world's artistic heritage, but also a reminder of the dangers and complexities that art faces when it intersects with greed, crime, and mystery.

32. Captain Kidd's Treasure: Legends and Mysteries of the Most Infamous Pirate

Captain William Kidd, better known as Captain Kidd, is an iconic figure of the age of piracy, whose legend is closely linked to the search for lost treasure. This treasure, supposedly hidden by Kidd before his capture, has intrigued historians, treasure hunters, and adventurers for centuries.

Captain Kidd's treasure allegedly consists of gold, jewelry, coins, and other valuables accumulated during his raids in the Indian Ocean and the Atlantic. Some reports mention that Kidd was also carrying cargoes of silk, spices, and ivory, acquired during his attacks on merchant ships. This loot is believed to have been buried in several places but has never been found in its entirety.

William Kidd began his career as a private captain, hired by the British Crown to protect maritime trade and attack enemy ships. However, his reputation quickly changed when he was accused of piracy after plundering the Armenian ship Quedagh Merchant in 1698.

To protect himself from prosecution, Kidd allegedly hid some of his loot in remote locations, including the famous Gardiners Island, near Long Island, New York. He was arrested in 1699, put on trial in England, and executed in 1701. The existence of the treasure became a crucial element of his trial, but Kidd never revealed its location, thus fueling the myth of his lost fortune.

Over the years, numerous searchers have attempted to locate Kidd's treasure. Some key points related to your search include:

Gardiners Island (New York): In 1699, Kidd supposedly buried a treasure chest on this island. Later, the British authorities recovered a portion of this treasure, confirming Kidd's practice of hiding his loot.

Caribbean Islands: Several legends suggest that Kidd would have buried treasures on islands such as Culebra and Hispaniola (present-day Dominican Republic and Haiti).

Madagascar: As a haven for pirates, this island is frequently mentioned in connection with Kidd. Some believe that he hid treasures there before leaving for North America.

Scotland: Kidd was born in Dundee, Scotland, and some theorists have suggested that he may have hidden part of his button in his homeland.

Some argue that much of the treasure was recovered by British authorities or looted by other pirates.

Some think that the magnitude of Kidd's treasure was exaggerated and that it could have been much smaller than the legends suggest.

Interesting facts:

In 2007, a team of explorers claimed to have found the wreckage of the Quedagh Merchant off the coast of the Dominican Republic. Although some artifacts were recovered, no significant riches were found.

The story of Kidd and his treasure has inspired numerous novels, films, and television series, making him a symbol of the golden age of piracy.

Kidd's trial was one of the first to use evidence of the burial of treasure as evidence against a pirate, setting legal precedents for future transactions.

Captain Kidd's treasure remains a captivating mystery that combines history, myth, and adventure. Their quest not only reflects the human longing to find material riches but also to discover fragments of the past that connect with the fascination with pirates and their world. Is it lost or is it lying hidden waiting to be found? Only the time and effort of search engines will be able to answer this question.